Attacking Soccer

Joseph A. Luxbacher
Editor

Human Kinetics

Library of Congress Cataloging-in-Publication Data

Luxbacher, Joe.
   Attacking soccer / Joseph A. Luxbacher, editor.
      p.   cm.
   ISBN 0-7360-0123-9
   1. Soccer--Offense.   2. Soccer--Training   I. Title.
   GV943.9.D43L88   1999
   796.334'2--dc21

99-28703
CIP

ISBN: 0-7360-0123-9

Copyright © 1999 by Human Kinetics Publishers, Inc.

Acquisitions Editor: Jeff Riley; **Managing Editor:** Leigh LaHood; **Copyeditor:** Bob Replinger; **Proofreader:** Andrew Smith; **Graphic Designer:** Fred Starbird; **Graphic Artist:** Tara Welsch; **Cover Designer:** Jack W. Davis; **Photographer (cover):** © Action Images; **Illustrator:** Tom Roberts; **Printer:** Versa Press

Human Kinetics books are available at special discounts for bulk purchase. Special editions or book excerpts can also be created to specification. For details, contact the Special Sales Manager at Human Kinetics.

Printed in the United States of America   10 9 8 7 6 5 4 3 2 1

Human Kinetics
Web site: http://www.humankinetics.com/

United States: Human Kinetics
P.O. Box 5076
Champaign, IL 61825-5076
1-800-747-4457
e-mail: humank@hkusa.com

Canada: Human Kinetics
475 Devonshire Road Unit 100
Windsor, ON N8Y 2L5
1-800-465-7301 (in Canada only)
e-mail: humank@hkcanada.com

Europe: Human Kinetics
P.O. Box IW14
Leeds LS16 6TR, United Kingdom
+44 (0) 113-278 1708
e-mail: humank@hkeurope.com

Australia: Human Kinetics
57A Price Avenue
Lower Mitcham, South Australia 5062
(08) 82771555
e-mail: humank@hkaustralia.com

New Zealand: Human Kinetics
P.O. Box 105-231
Auckland Central
09-523-3462
e-mail: humank@hknewz.com

Contents

Drill Finder

continued

Key to Diagrams

X	Any player
S	Server
GK	Goalkeeper
RB	Right back
LB	Left back
CB	Center back
RMF	Right midfielder
LMF	Left midfielder
CMF	Central midfielder
AMF	Attacking midfielder
DMF	Defending midfielder
MF	Any midfielder
RFW	Right forward
LFW	Left forward
CFW	Central forward
F	Any forward
T	Target player
A	Attacker
D	Defender
N	Neutral player
⟶	Path of player
⇢	Path of the ball
∿⟶	Path of player dribbling the ball

Acknowledgments

Although I have authored several books, this is my first effort at editing one. I found the process to be quite interesting and also came to the realization that successful completion of such a project truly requires a team effort. I am therefore greatly indebted to a number of individuals for their assistance in bringing to fruition my original idea of a book focused on attacking soccer. Although it is not possible to mention everyone by name, I would like to express my sincere appreciation to the following individuals.

- The outstanding staff at Human Kinetics, particularly Jeff Riley and Leigh LaHood, for lending their support and expertise in the development of the book.
- My coaching colleagues who graciously contributed chapters to the book, for their exceptional work as well as their willingness to share knowledge and expertise with coaches and players at all levels of competition.

Special mention goes to my mother, Mary Ann Luxbacher, who, in her eighth decade of life, still provides unwavering support and encouragement for everything that I do. Most importantly, I want to thank my beautiful wife, Gail, for her constant love, support, and patience, particularly when the writing takes place during the wee hours of the morning or late hours of the evening. She, along with our daughter, Eliza Gail, and young son, Travis Joseph, are my steadfast source of happiness and inspiration, a constant reminder that the most important experiences in life do not occur on the athletic field.

The Fundamentals of Attacking Soccer

The game of soccer is in a constant state of evolution. Each World Cup tournament unveils innovations in tactics and systems of play. Despite the changing nature of the game, certain concepts of team attack remain constant—basic fundamentals that apply to all systems and styles of play. Part I discusses the fundamentals of attacking soccer in the different thirds of the field.

The initial stage of team attack often begins in the defending third of the field nearest a team's goal. Play may originate from the goalkeeper as he or she distributes the ball to a teammate after making a save, or from a defender who, having tackled the ball from an opposing forward, makes an outlet pass to begin the counterattack. Regardless of the scenario, the ability of a team to advance the ball swiftly and effectively out of the defending third provides the foundation for successful attacking soccer.

In chapter 1 Dave Masur of St. John's University provides a blueprint for effectively playing the ball out of the defending third. Coaches commonly refer to this section of the field as the area of no risk because loss of possession here can prove disastrous. It is essential that a team be able to advance the ball safely and effectively out of their defending third. Some teams do this through short- and medium-distance *possession passes*. Others prefer a more straightforward style of play, bypassing the midfield by serving the ball directly into front-running target players. Both methods will work if executed properly. The key to success is to play simple and play safe.

In chapter 2 John Kowalski, present coach of the Pittsburgh Riverhounds (A League) and formerly of the Tampa Bay Mutiny (MLS), discusses how to advance the ball swiftly and safely through the midde third of the field. This section of the field is generally regarded as an area of moderate risk. Dribbling skills are used here with greater frequency and with more positive results than in the defending third of the field, although effective combination play is still the rule rather than the exception. Coach Kowalski provides a series of game-simulated drills that reflect his knowledge and expertise in laying the groundwork for creative midfield play.

In chapter 3 University at Buffalo coach John Astudillo addresses the question of how to create quality scoring chances in the attacking third of the field. The emphasis here is on *quality* chances, on creating scoring situations in the most dangerous scoring zones—front and center of the goal. Scoring goals regularly at the highest levels requires much more than brilliant individual play. Granted, natural talent is an essential part of the equation, but it must be coupled with collective team play. Against well-organized defenses, players must work together, and in some cases for one another, to create quality opportunities. The objective is to create opportunities that provide a wide shooting angle to goal. Coach Astudillo provides a series of drills predicated on that theme.

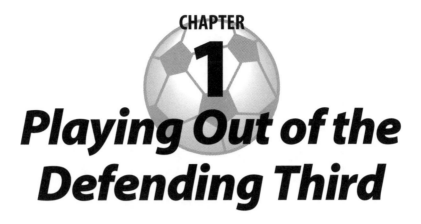

Playing Out of the Defending Third

Dave Masur

St. John's University

A team can use a variety of methods to play out of its defensive third of the field. The wind, the condition of the field, the strengths of its players, its game plan or style, and the opponent and its defensive strategy all affect the strategies that a team might use. This chapter will examine each style of playing out of the back, give you a brief overview, and provide drills that pertain to that style.

Direct Play From Punting or Goal Kicks

Goalkeepers and defenders will sometimes need to drive the ball high, far, and deep down the center of the field to gain quality field position for their team. The offensive team will generally use this tactic in the beginning of the game, with one or two minutes before halftime, and near the end of the game. This tactic provides opportunities to win second balls in midfield or air balls by flicking a header behind the other team's defense for an onrushing attack!

1 Shadow Play

Have goalkeepers and defenders drive balls down the center of the field to your target players. The rest of the team should squeeze up and in to make the game compact. Add defensive players for resistance.

Key Points

- Encourage players to win first header.
- Players should time runs behind the defense to win the ball.
- Players should squeeze space and be prepared to win second ball off defensive header.
- Players should keep the game compact and be safe at the back with direct play!

continued

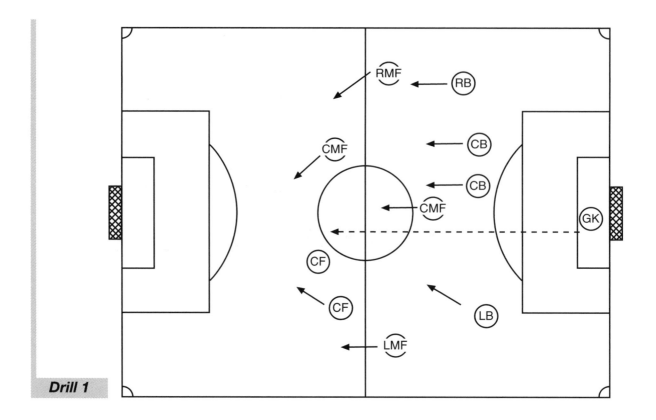

Drill 1

Playing to Feet in Midfield

This tactic requires a team to be quick with skills and decision making. Your midfield players need to create spaces so they or their teammates can check back to receive the ball. The midfield player should look to turn or make a quick pass to an appropriate supporting player, who should be at the proper angle and spacing.

2 Playing Out of Back (4 vs. 3)

Play four offensive players, generally your four defenders, vs. three defenders from the opposing team in your defensive third of the field. Play three touch to increase support and ball movement in the defensive third. The team with the ball is looking to play balls through an open channel into the midfielders' feet. Once the ball is played out of the defensive third into midfield, the midfielders must turn and find the forwards in the offensive third of the field. This drill will enhance your team's ability to play in tight spaces in the defensive third of the field.

continued

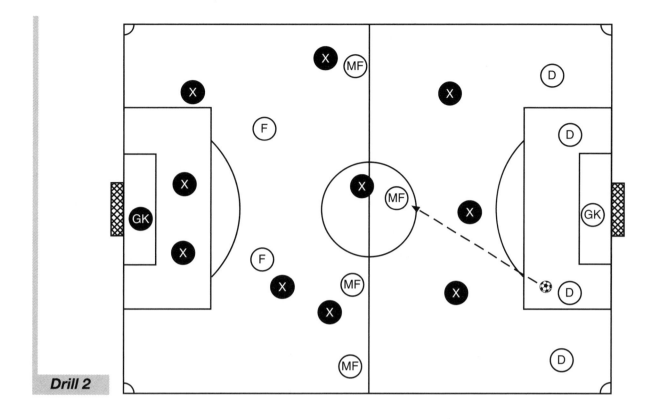

Drill 2

Switching the Point of Attack at the Back

After your defenders learn to create channels and develop direct play into midfield, it's time to work on spreading your defenders wide, developing the play on one side of the field, and then switching the ball to an opposite outside back overlapping into a wide midfield position. You accomplish this by holding the ball using your central defender, midfield player, and outside back on one side of the field and then quickly switching the point of attack to the other side.

Your defenders must be good at accurately driving the ball over a distance to another defender. Switching play by driving the ball to the outside back simulates overlapping passes and receptions. The drill provides functional training for defenders on driving and receiving long passes.

Using the same drill, have the defenders work the ball out of the back against three forwards who are applying pressure on them. The key is to move the ball constantly from one side of the field to the other before identifying an overlapping pass or switch! Add one or two midfield players on both offense and defense to provide additional options in switching the point of attack.

The objective is to build confidence on the ball and develop quality decision making in recognizing and executing a switch of the field by your defense to an overlapping defender.

Clipping Serves Into Feet

An overlooked skill that defenders must possess is the ability to clip a service over the midfield and drop a soft pass into a forward's feet. Defenders too often drive balls or otherwise deliver balls poorly to their forwards. The supply of quality balls from your backs is essential to the success of your team.

3 Direct Play: Back to Front

Divide the field into thirds and have four defenders being pressured at 75 percent by four forwards. Under this pressure the defenders must create space for themselves off the dribble and then clip a quality serve over the midfield third into the feet of one of their forwards. Forwards will be marked (but only goal side) by their defenders. After this add midfield players to the middle third. They may cut out any service that is too low. Keep score of good execution of passes. You may use two balls and develop the drill to go back and forth with both sides serving and receiving.

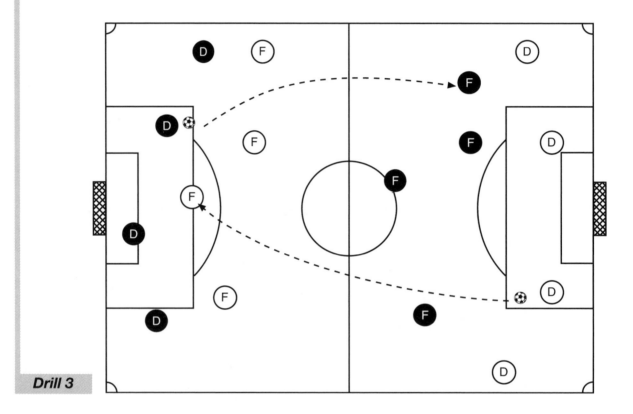

Drill 3

Playing the Ball Behind the Defense

An important method of starting the attack relies on the ability of your defenders to make passes to forwards or midfielders making well-timed runs behind the other team's defense or into flank spaces. This type of execution takes a properly angled, well-timed run and an accurate pass with a little cushion so the ball slows up for the onrushing attacks.

4 Behind the Defense

Set up a drill so that your team is entering the midfield area and is not quite into the attacking third. When a player makes a pass to a supporting defender, the team should look to make runs to free one of their players behind the opposing team's defense.

In this diagram the central midfielder plays the ball back to the left back. The left forward checks into a space, looking for the ball into his or her feet. The left forward, however, has created a space for the right-side forward to make a run across the field and into the space behind the defense. They should continue to finish the play to goal with all players joining in.

By working diligently on this exercise, your team can learn to exploit several avenues and develop many patterns of play. For instance, you can look to get both outside midfielders behind the defense, or the center midfielder into striking position, with well-timed runs. Even overlapping defenders can make runs behind the defense. Use this exercise to expand your team's offensive timing.

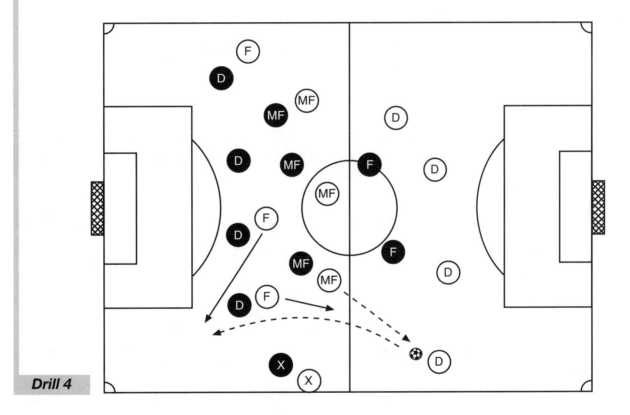

Drill 4

Conclusion

As you can see, a team can use many ways to deliver the ball from their back third of the field. What works best for your team will depend on your coaching and your team's playing style, but your players should be competent in all areas—direct play, playing to midfielders' feet, switching the point of attack, clipping serves to forwards, and playing balls behind the defense or to channels. These overall themes can make your team diverse and unpredictable.

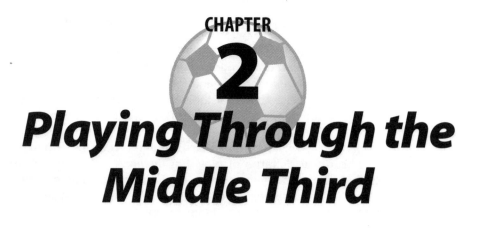

2

Playing Through the Middle Third

John Kowalski

Pittsburgh Riverhounds

Soccer in the '90s is played in many styles and systems. The systems of play, formations, strategies, and styles vary greatly from country to country, as shown in the 1998 World Cup in France. Some teams are highly organized tactically and play "mechanically." These teams use the same patterns repeatedly, especially in the buildup and the attack through the midfield. Some teams are scientific and play direct soccer. Other teams are organized with a common understanding in midfield tactics.

A special playmaker, an attacking midfielder, is many times referred to as "number 10." Carlos Valderamma typifies the number 10. He is an excellent passer, with great touch and vision. He plays in the midfield like a conductor leading an orchestra, establishing the rhythm and directing his teammates through their parts of the symphony. His work rate off the ball is high. He finds himself in excellent positions in central midfield to distribute the ball and make many assists.

Marco Etcheverry is also an excellent passer, especially in changing the point of attack, and a good penetrating dribbler. His work rate is good, and he is able to lead his team from a central midfield position to many goal-scoring chances and team wins.

Preki is a talented playmaking midfielder as well. He can improvise and make penetrating dribbles. Preki likes to shoot from long range, which makes him extremely dangerous.

The midfield is the heart of the team. Playing the midfield requires stamina, endurance, ability to play under pressure, and an understanding of different phases of the game. The midfielder must be an all-around player, capable of playing effectively both in the attack and on defense. It is essential that the midfield players understand what is required in any part of the field at different stages of the game.

Necessary Tools: Ball Control and Passing

The techniques and skills necessary to become an effective midfield player are vision, ball control, passing, dribbling, and stamina. Above all, the midfielder must be quick in controlling the ball, preparing it, and passing it accurately. The midfielder, often surrounded by opponents, usually uses two or three touches to take control and prepare the ball. In some situations the midfielder will not have time to bring the ball under control and must be able to make the first-time pass to a supporting teammate. Other times he or she must be creative and able to improvise.

Protecting the Ball and Dribbling

Because many players are usually nearby, a good midfield player must be able to hold and screen the ball to make time for himself or herself and for teammates. The midfielder should be able to dribble and pass to set up teammates who are in a better position to carry out an attack or score. The ability to make penetrating dribbles and runs with the ball that will play opponents out of their defensive postures is an important aspect of midfield play.

Midfielders playing wide should be able to cross the ball effectively and connect with the strikers. Accurate shooting from long range is also highly desirable. Tackling and taking balls away are components of every midfielder's defensive play.

In this chapter I will show you drills and small-sided games that will help you train your midfield players. These drills, designed and used by international and MLS teams, are beneficial for players 15 years old and older who have basic technical skills under control.

5   Warm-Up

Purpose

To improve ability to maintain ball possession and change the point of attack.

Organization

Use markers to outline two 12-by-15-yard rectangles about 25 yards apart. Organize two teams of 7 to 10 players each, one team in each rectangle. A coach or server sets up about 10 or 15 yards away with 8 to 12 balls.

Procedure

1. A coach or server passes a ball to the players in rectangle A.

2. Players in rectangle A must make seven consecutive passes. To score one point, a long pass in the air must land in rectangle B.

3. After the coach or server passes the ball to rectangle A, two players from rectangle B run to interrupt or recover the ball before the A players can complete their seven passes or make the long pass.

4. Should the A players score, the game continues with the B players making seven consecutive passes and the long pass. Meanwhile two of their teammates return to rectangle B and two A players run to rectangle B to interrupt or recover the ball.

continued

Key Points

- If the A team cannot complete seven passes or send an accurate pass in the air to the opposite rectangle, then the coach or server restarts the game by passing the next ball, and the game continues. (Players must occasionally recover balls.)
- Play up to five points or 15 to 20 minutes.

Variation

Limit players to one touch.

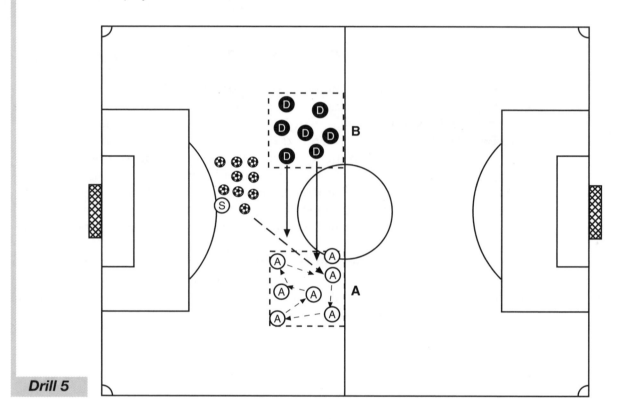

Drill 5

6   Warm-Up Technical and Tactical

Purpose

To improve ball-possession skills, passing under pressure, support runs, and technical ability.

Organization

Use markers to outline a playing area of 44 by 36 yards. Organize three teams of four players each.

Procedure

1. Play 4 vs. 4 with four support players outside the playing area, one on each side of the rectangle.
2. Limit the support players to one or two touches.
3. Change the team on the outside every three to five minutes.

continued

Key Point

Players in the playing area should use the support players for wall passing, overlap runs, and takeovers.

Variation

Limit the players in the playing area to two touches.

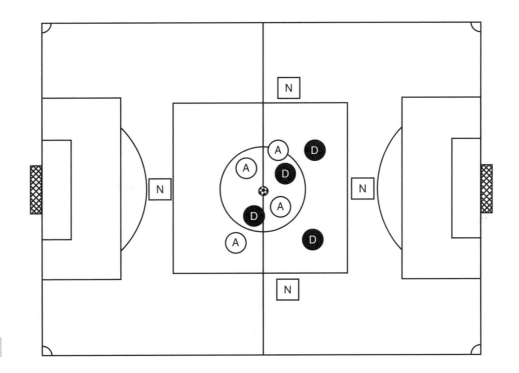

Drill 6

7 Numbers-Up Attacking

Purpose

To develop flow in penetrating through the middle zone.

Organization

Use a field space of 36 by 32 yards. Organize two teams of four players each. Play 4 vs. 4 with two neutral players who always play with the team in possession of the ball.

Procedure

1. Each team defends one end line.

2. To score, a player must dribble over the end line and maintain ball possession.

Key Points

- Players should move the ball, circulate the ball, and open the space.
- Look for accurate passing.

Variation

To score, a player must receive a pass and control the ball within one step of the end line.

continued

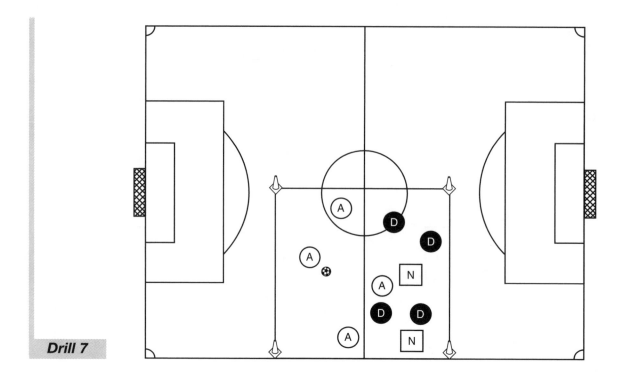

Drill 7

8   3 vs. 3 vs. 3

Purpose

To improve support and ball possession, and understand numerical advantage.

Organization

Use a field space of 44 by 30 yards. Organize three teams of three players each. Play 6 vs. 3 for 15 to 20 minutes.

Procedure

1. To start, two teams play keep away vs. the third.

2. The third team, upon recovery of the ball, plays numbers up.

3. The team whose player lost possession of the ball is the next team in the middle.

Key Point

Players should provide support without the ball, so the player on the ball always has the possibility for left or right passes, short passes, or long passes up the middle.

Variations

- Play 4 vs. 4 vs. 4.
- Play on a bigger or smaller field.
- Limit players to two touches.

Drill 8

9 5 vs. 3 Ball Possession

Purpose

To improve conditioning, playing under pressure, and ball-possession ability.

Organization

Use a field space of 18 by 44 yards (the size of the penalty area). Organize two teams, an attacking team of five players and a defending team of three players.

Procedure

1. The attacking team of five players gets the ball. They play three touch or two touch.
2. The defending team of three players attempts to recover the ball. Upon recovering it, they have unlimited touches.
3. To score, the attacking team must make 10 consecutive passes without the defending team gaining possession.
4. To score, the defending team must make six consecutive passes.
5. Play a five-minute game, and then change players.

Key Point

Players should keep the ball moving.

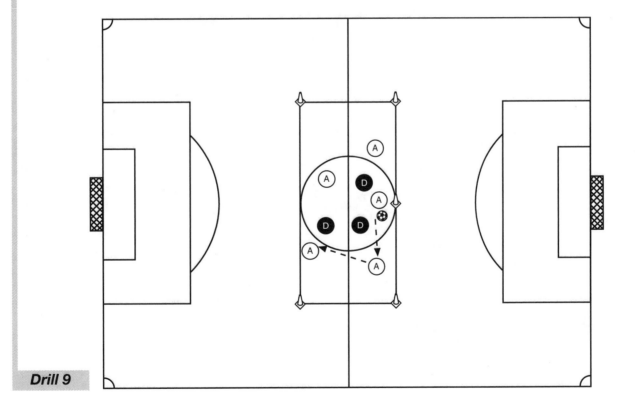

Drill 9

10 10-Gates Game

Purpose

To improve dribbling, passing, and combination play.

Organization

Use cones 2 yards apart to set up 10 gates. Place them randomly on a field of 40 by 55 yards. Organize two teams of eight players. Play 8 vs. 8 for 20 minutes.

Procedure

To score, a player must dribble through a gate.

Key Point

Players should move the ball.

Variations

- To score, players pass the ball through a gate.
- Limit players to two touches.

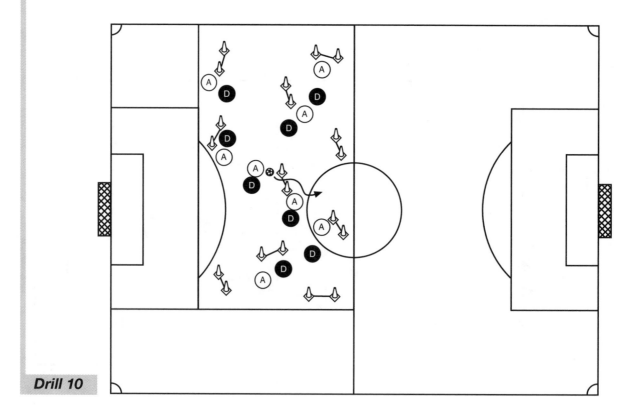

Drill 10

11 End-Zone Game

Purpose

To attack through the middle channel with proper support and balance.

Organization

Use a field space of 44 by 36 yards with a 2- to 3-yard end zone at each end of the field. Organize two teams of four players each.

Procedure

1. The teams attack opposite end zones.
2. To score, a player must dribble through the end line and control the ball in the end zone.
3. Play for 20 minutes.

Key Point

Players must move the ball.

Variations

- To score, a player must receive and control a passed ball in the end zone.
- Play 5 vs. 5.

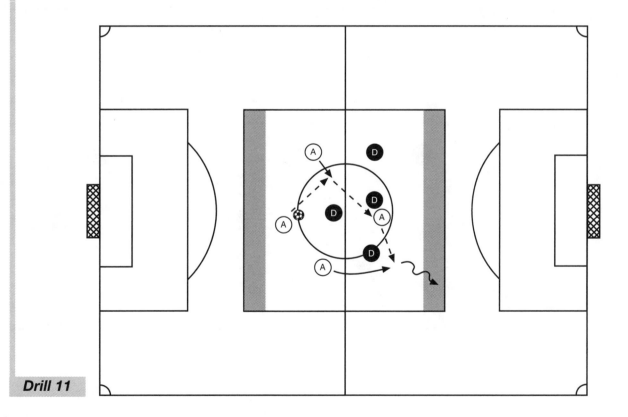

Drill 11

12 Changing the Point of Attack I

Purpose

To build up the attack, change the point of attack, use vision, and provide support without the ball.

Organization

Use four small goals, three to five yards wide. Set up two on the center line and two on the edge of the penalty area. Organize two teams and play 7 vs. 7.

Procedure

1. Play a game of 15 to 20 minutes with unlimited touches.

2. Each team defends two goals.

3. One team defends the two goals on the center line; the other defends the two goals along the 18-yard line.

Variations

• Play 6 vs. 6 or 8 vs. 8.

• Limit players to two touches.

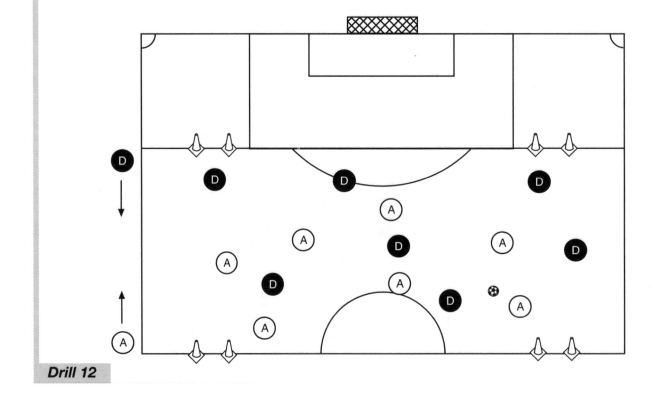

Drill 12

(13) Changing the Point of Attack II

Purpose

To build up the attack and change the point of attack.

Organization

Organize two teams. The attacking team has six players, two strikers and four midfielders. The defending team has five field players, three defenders and two midfielders, plus two goalkeepers. Set up three small goals marked with cones on the center line and two regular-size goals along the six-yard box.

Procedure

1. The attacking team attacks the two big goals and defends the three small goals.
2. The defending team defends the two big goals and attacks the three small goals.
3. Play 20 to 25 minutes.

Key Points

- The attacking team tries to build up to score. The midfielders must penetrate going forward or make combination plays to score.
- Teams should maintain balance in numbers so they can change the point of attack using long diagonal air balls to score at the weak-side goal.
- Upon losing ball possession, teams should maintain balance for defensive transitions, pressure, ball recovery, or defending.

Variations

- The defending team has six field players—four defenders and two midfielders—plus two goalkeepers. The attacking team has seven players—three forwards and four midfielders.
- Play the same game but limit players to two touches.

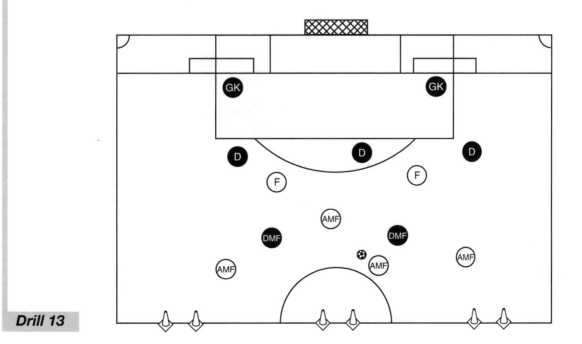

Drill 13

14 Combination Play and Crossing Game

Purpose

To improve overlap runs, crosses, and attacking runs from strikers and midfielders.

Organization

Organize two teams of six field players and a goalkeeper. Two neutral players take positions in the wide channels. Play on half a field with two regular goals.

Procedure

1. The goalkeeper distributes the ball to a teammate.
2. After the team makes three consecutive passes without the opposing team touching the ball, a player can pass to a neutral support player in the wide channel.
3. After making the pass, the passer executes an overlap run.
4. After receiving the return pass, the overlapping player crosses the ball.
5. Six players play attack and defense, making attacking runs.

Key Points

- During the overlap run, the player must look up.
- Players must time the crosses.
- Players must time the attacking runs.

Variation

Takeovers by the supporting attacker in the wide channel (where a neutral player is stationed) follow with a dribble and cross.

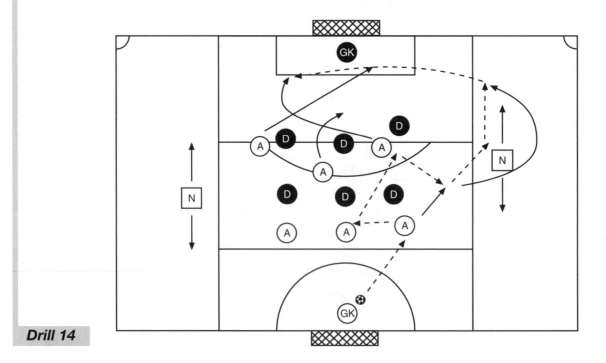

15 Crossing Game

Purpose

To improve crossing and finishing crosses under game conditions.

Organization

Organize two teams of six field players and a goalkeeper. Four neutral players, two on each side, play as wide midfielders. The teams play 6 vs. 6 through the middle channel on half a field with two regular goals and marked penalty areas.

Procedure

1. The goalkeeper distributes the ball wide (alternating left and right).
2. The two neutral players on each side are free (no defenders). They must execute a passing combination with a setup pass and then serve a quality cross.
3. Six field players make timed runs to the near side, far side, and middle areas of the goal, trying to finish every cross on goal.
4. When a goal is scored or the ball goes out of bounds, the goalkeeper always restarts the game.
5. When the defending team intercepts the ball, they distribute the ball wide and the game continues.

Key Point

Players should originate crosses in or near the edge of the penalty area.

Variation

Use inswinging crosses and outswinging crosses.

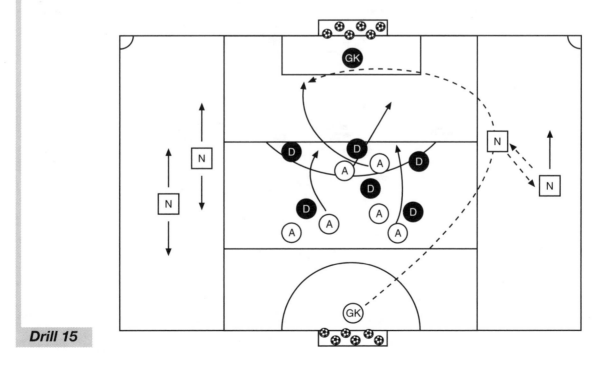

Drill 15

16 Pressing to Score

Purpose

To play with the pressure of having to score quickly.

Organization

Organize two teams, each with eight players and a goalkeeper. Play on a half field with two regular goals.

Procedure

1. The teams each defend a goal.
2. The visiting team holds a 1-0 lead with 10 minutes left in the game.
3. The home team is attacking.
4. After 10 minutes change roles.

Key Points

- Players should observe defensive principles by giving immediate chase and getting goal side.
- The defending team should apply pressure to win the ball.
- Teams should work on quick transition, direct attacking, and putting the ball in the danger zone quickly.

Variation

Play with five minutes left in the game.

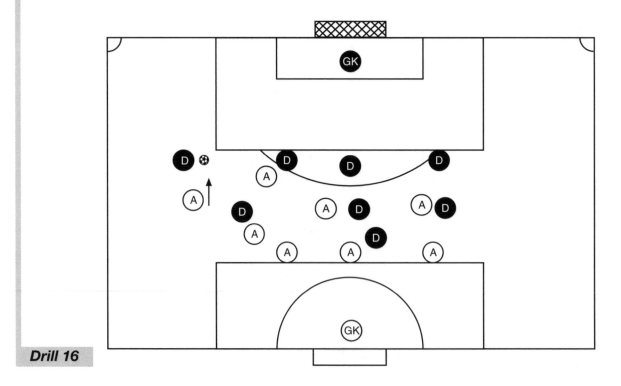

3

Creating Opportunities in the Attacking Third

John Astudillo
University at Buffalo

A prerequisite for scoring is commitment by a team to score. Although a team should give some thought to defending, in case they lose the ball, all 11 players must adopt the mentality that the next stop is the back of the net. The players must be in synch emotionally and aware of the next tactical reaction by a player or group of players.

Teams in position to enter the final third of the field have several options. These include

- creating player movement with and without the ball,
- creating space for ball carriers or players waiting to receive the ball, and
- creating time for players with the ball, enabling them to be a scoring threat.

Although some goals are the result of unending improvisation, coaches must teach and condition their teams to recognize certain elements of attack—even improvisation needs training. Brazilians often train certain patterns of attack that they feel will help them during matches. Often they integrate samba music into their training routine to break up the dullness of repetition and maintain a spirited attacking ambiance during the session. Of greater importance, however, is establishing and maintaining a sense of attacking cohesiveness and rhythm.

Establish the mood of the match from the outset by urging the team to probe immediately for weak points in the other team's defense. The flanks, the middle, the ground, and the air should be considered avenues of attack. When probes in these areas have occurred, a team may settle into repeating the conditions and opportunities for attack. In South America the large partisan crowds begin to chant "Ahí viene el gol," meaning "Here comes the goal," because they have sensed that some or all of these conditions are in place to score.

For goals to occur, the team or the ball must penetrate deep into the final third. Relying on long-distance shots is not uncommon, but goalkeepers today are so good that they will usually deny you this option. Instead you should train and practice penetration. In the final third, penetration can occur with the ball being sent or with a player carrying the ball.

Let's look at the different ways to attack the final third.

1. Individual dribbling should be encouraged at the sight of free space. Players with the ball on a 1 vs. 1 must learn to attack if the defender is unsupported. The diagram on page 23 shows several options and angles of attack and finish. In developing young soccer players, coaches are not spending enough time teaching players to be dribblers and to take on unsupported defenders at every opportunity. A coach should be as critical of a player for not recognizing and taking on an unsupported 1 vs. 1 as for ignoring an opportunity to pass for a score. Coaches must train players individually and as a group to create, recognize, and execute opportunities to score when they have arrived in the attacking third.

2. Players escorting and supporting the player with the ball can be trained on the several options of combining from different angles and distances from the goal. Combination play must occur at this point, with getting behind the defense the first priority. The diagrams on pages 24 and 25 show several options for combination play by two or three players in a limited area.

3. Players at midfield as a group must be trained to set up a weak-side play with *east-west movement*. Start play on one flank and quickly switch the point of attack with either diagonal or lateral balls to the player on the opposite (weak) side. The diagrams on pages 26, 27, and 28 show the conditions necessary to create the opportunity to score on the weak side. The players who will be penetrating the final third will be either lateral players (middies) or back players (defenders).

4. Players at the forward and midfield lines must also be trained in the intricacies of combination play in a *north-south direction*. The diagram on page 29 shows the many variations of this movement. This series should include movement of players laterally as well as switching of position by attackers and midfielders to keep the defense unbalanced. The movement of players will also produce positive space for other players to attack.

5. All players in the forward, middle, and back positions should be trained to integrate themselves into the attack. The diagram on page 30 demonstrates the final progression of all integrated lines. Train the team through repetition on certain patterns of attack. Shadow training without defenders should be the first step. Add defenders progressively as effectiveness increases and players more easily recognize and execute patterns.

Unless a team is blessed with many offensive-minded players, the coach must create a commitment to attack. Players will play with more concentration and enjoyment if they are part of the larger scheme of attacking. Although playing defense is enjoyable, soccer players love to score. Training should be devoted to attacking until they score. Attacking individually, in small groups, or as a team is the way for a team to remain unpredictable and score more goals.

17 Individual Attacking

Purpose

To train attackers to recognize unsupported defenders and attack them immediately.

Organization

Use four stations throughout the field with goals and goalkeepers on as many goals as possible. Set up cones at (a) 20 yards and a 120 degree-angle from goal, (b) 15 yards and a 90-degree angle from goal, (c) 25 yards and a 150-degree angle from goal, and (d) 10 yards and a 90-degree angle from goal. Use servers with an extra ball behind each net. Attackers should be forwards, midfielders, and, if necessary, attacking backs.

Procedure

1. Player A takes on a defender in station A, then moves on to stations B, C, and finally to D. The player must engage the defender, beat him or her, and take a shot.

2. The server throws another ball to the attacker, who moves to the next station. The server retrieves the other ball.

Key Points

- Attackers must understand that certain moves will work better at certain angles.
- From a central position a single "Matthews" will be effective.
- From an extreme-angle position, a sharp inside cut combined with a stepover will be effective.

Variations

- Encourage players to use both single moves and combination moves.
- Train players to use different speeds as they approach the defender.

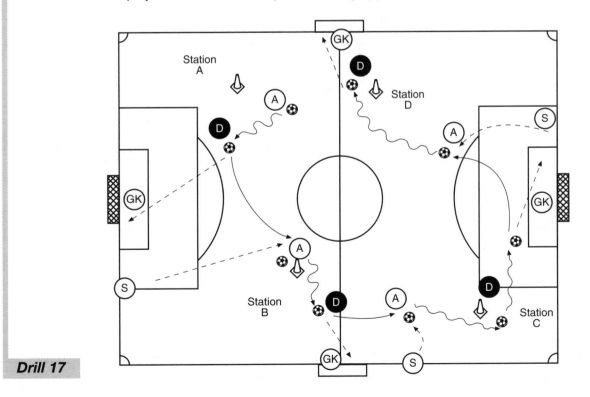

Drill 17

18 Attacking With One and Two Supporting Players

Purpose

To train reacting with one or two other attacking players.

Organization

In a 25-by-30-yard area, three players attack and weave for quick passing and shooting 20 yards from a goal. Set up stations A, B, and C so that attacking players can move continuously from one station to another.

Procedure

Three players execute the following patterns:

1. Player A_A dribbles diagonally and passes laterally to player A_B, who dribbles diagonally and then passes diagonally to player A_C, who passes to player A_A for a shot.

2. Player A_A passes the ball vertically to player A_B, who passes the ball vertically to player A_C, who also executes a vertical pass to player A_A for a shot on goal.

3. Player A_A passes the ball diagonally to player A_B and overlaps player A_B on the flank. Player A_B dribbles the ball laterally in the opposite direction and passes the ball diagonally to incoming player A_C. Player A_C then passes the ball to overlapping player A_A for a shot.

Key Points

- These exercises train supporting players to make runs in support of the ball. The runs should be in anticipation of, and in reaction to, movement of the ball.

- Train players in the different types of runs—bent, diagonal, and vertical.

- Emphasize the pace and angle of the runs to prevent offsides. Equally important is the position of the run on the inside or on the flank.

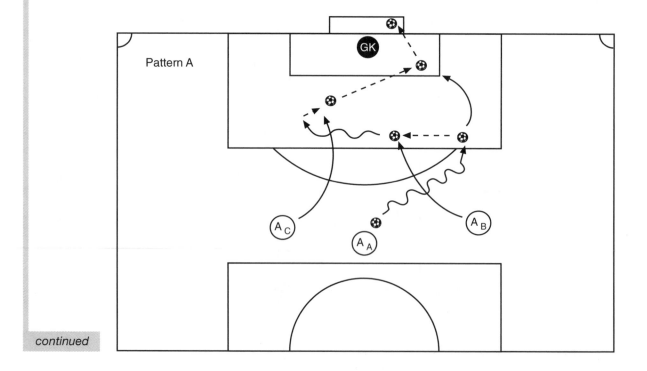

Pattern A

continued

Variations

- Encourage players to progress from two touches to one touch.
- Increase the speed of the drill as players become proficient.

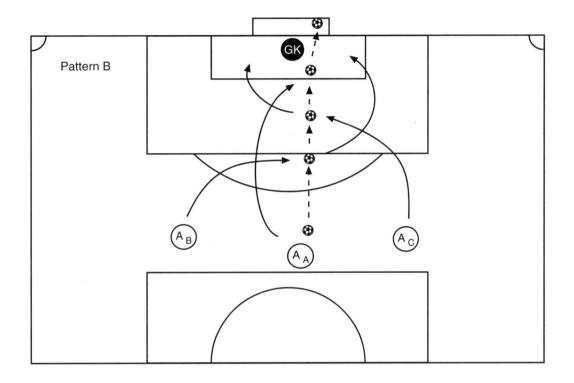

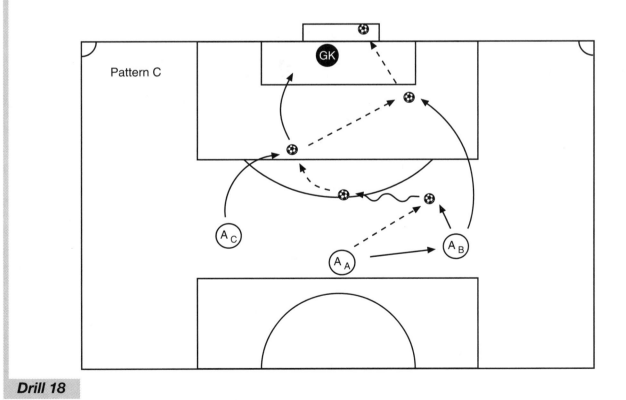

Drill 18

19 Attacking With Midfielders

Purpose

To train attackers to recognize numbers and attack on the flank and the box.

Organization

Play a 4 vs. 2 keep-away game for 30 seconds.

Procedure

1. Play in the middle of the field.

2. Players must play one or two touches only.

3. When the players execute five consecutive one-touch passes, a midfielder in a back position joins in.

Key Points

- This progressive exercise teaches the midfielders to play quickly. As they connect passes they gain numbers from the back.

- Encourage passes through the middle.

- Movement of the ball should be designed and executed with vision of the flanks. When the extra flank player joins the attack, the penetrating pass should have the proper angle for vision.

Variations

- Play a 5 vs. 2 and then a 5 vs. 3 as the attack becomes more proficient.

- On five consecutive one touches, allow two flank players rather than one. They should make themselves available at either flank and force the midfielder to make a choice.

- Have a back defender waiting for the attackers as a deep back.

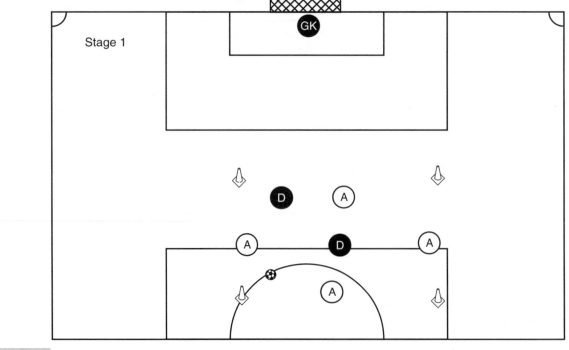

continued

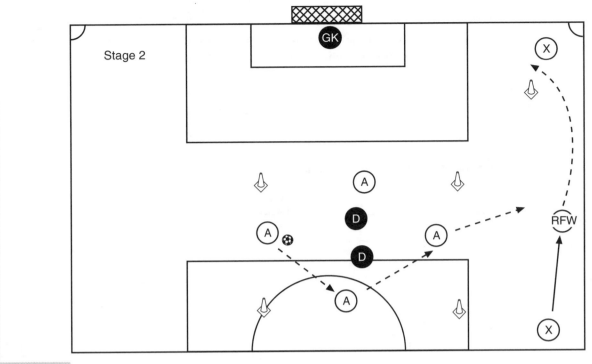

Drill 19

20 Attacking With Midfielders by Changing Points of Attack

Purpose

To train attacking middies to attack by changing the points of attack.

Organization

Play 8 vs. 8 + 2 with six goals set up in the middle of the field and three clearly marked zones.

Procedure

1. Two teams play 8 vs. 8 in half of the field. Limit players to two touches in the central zone but allow multiple touches in the free zones on the flanks.

2. The team with the ball has a +2 advantage so they can switch to the other side when defenders close down the space.

3. Teams cannot score unless they touch all three zones at least once. Central goals are worth five points and flank goals three points.

Key Points

- This exercise trains attacking players in the middle zones to exploit the weak-side flank as an avenue of attack.

- Players in the central zone must play quickly and receive the ball with an open stance to their weak side if possible.

continued

- Emphasize simple and quick passing for possession and control.
- Players learn to open up defenses by forcing the defense to cover the width, thus allowing scoring opportunities in the central goals.

Variations

- If not enough goals are being scored, introduce a +3 player advantage.
- For more proficient players, encourage one touch in the central zone and count every one touch as one point.
- Require the team to cover all three zones twice before a score.

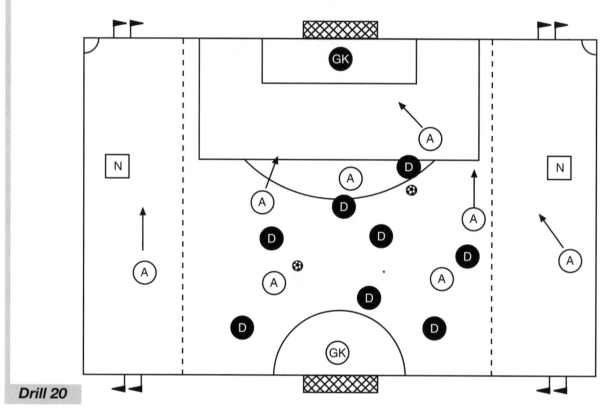

Drill 20

---

21 Attacking With Forwards and Midfielders

Purpose

To train the integration of midfielders and forwards into the attack as a group.

Organization

Use five midfielders with two attackers in a 30-by-70-yard area. Mark off a flank safe area of 10 yards for service and penetration only.

Procedure

1. Establish a ball-movement pattern in which the central midfielder serves a ball to the flank midfielder,
2. who is checking to the ball and who turns and passes the ball to a forward,

continued

3. who is checking diagonally to the flank and then plays the ball diagonally back to the other central midfielder,

4. who plays laterally to the other central middle,

5. who steps up and serves the ball forward to the other checking forward,

6. who plays the ball to the other flank attacking middle,

7. who carries the ball deep into the flank and serves the ball.

8. After the deep run develops, all middies and forwards attack the box in unison.

Key Points

- Start play at a moderate pace so that players understand the development of play and positions.

- Players should react intuitively and make runs based on their position as the attacking run develops. Players closest to the ball should look for a far-post position, and players farthest from the ball should go to the near post. Players should also react to each other's positions.

Variations

- Establish the patterns depending on the strength or size of the forwards. Some patterns should include direct north-south balls to forwards. Patterns should also include passing between forwards if they are adept passers.

- Also, allow one, then two, and finally three defenders.

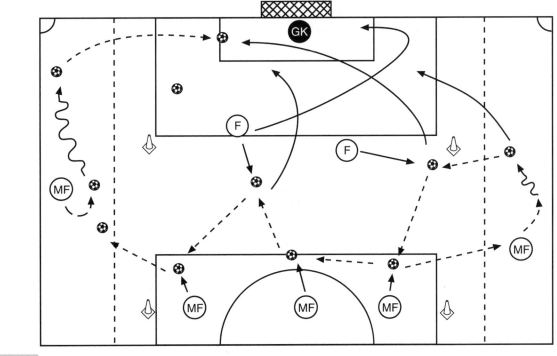

Drill 21

22 Attacking with Forwards, Midfielders, and Backs

Purpose

To train the integration of backs into the attacking third on the flank.

Organization

In the attacking third area of the field, mark two free areas on either flank: one as a midfielder corridor and one for the backs. Mark the area with a middle line. Play 4 vs. 4 with unlimited touch restrictions.

Procedure

1. Players play keepaway and attempt to move the ball between the middle areas.

2. When a team has successfully played the ball between areas A and B, it gains a midfielder in the next corridor and the area is expanded to include that corridor.

3. When the team has earned at least two extra middies, it can earn an extra back in the furthest corridor. The back carries the ball deep into the alley and serves.

4. As the back crosses the ball, attacking players attack the box, reacting to each other's runs.

Key Points

- This drill is designed to reveal deeper avenues of attack and additional support in the attack. Once a team has secured numbers through changes in the direction of attack, it must also consider the width of the field.

- Closely monitor the positioning of runs and modify when necessary. Players should know intuitively where to run.

Variation

Play 5 vs. 5 instead of 4 vs. 4.

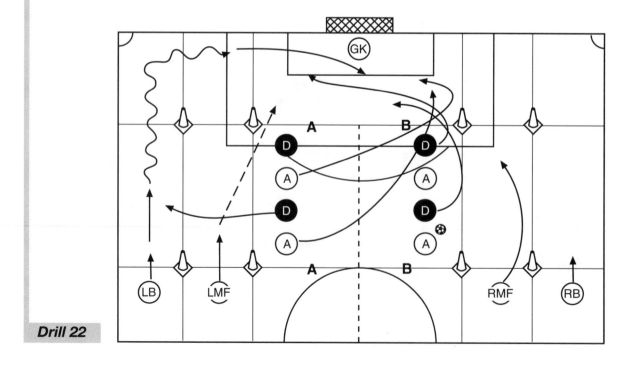

Drill 22

PART

II

Attacking Strategies and Tactics

The fundamental concepts discussed in part I apply to all systems and styles of play. The chapters in part II deal with strategies and tactics that teams may or may not use in their efforts to develop a strong attacking side. A team will usually establish its identity based on the nature and ability of its players, their level of expertise, and the coach's philosophy of play. As evidenced by the contrasting styles displayed during World Cup 1998, it is clear that teams can approach the game with different attacking philosophies. For example, nations like Denmark and Norway advocated a direct style of attack by serving long balls into deep-lying targets rather than playing through the midfield. In contrast, most of the South American qualifiers emphasized the possession game, advancing the ball through a succession of short- and medium-range passes. Teams like France, Holland, and Germany incorporated elements of both styles, meshing a ball-possession, tempo-dictating style of play with the ability to strike swiftly and suddenly when the opportunity presented itself. Part II discusses several of the more notable tactical and philosophical approaches to attacking soccer. Most teams try to incorporate two or more of these strategies into their attacking schemes.

In chapter 4 Dean Foti of Syracuse University illustrates the importance of ball possession and how teams can use it to create goal-scoring opportunities. It is obvious that a team will create few quality scoring opportunities if its players cannot withstand the attempts of opponents to dispossess them of the ball. Coach Foti uses a variety of exercises to develop possession play, drills that expose players to the situations they will face in game competition.

In chapter 5 Xavier University soccer coach Ron Quinn analyzes the tactic of changing the point of attack, the commonly accepted practice of constantly switching the location of the ball to attack the defense at its most vulnerable area. Coach Quinn provides a series of game-simulated activities that emphasize this all-important tactic.

In chapter 6 Dave Sarachan, assistant coach of MLS powerhouse D.C. United, demonstrates the importance of effective transition play. Teams are most vulnerable to swift counterattack during the moments immediately following loss of possession. Some teams base their entire attacking strategy on this fact. The instant a team gains possession of the ball, its players should shift immediately from a defensive safety-first orientation to a more aggressive attacking mentality. Coach Sarachan provides a series of drills to develop effective counterattack play.

Chapter 7 looks at attacking soccer from a somewhat different perspective—creating opportunities through effective flank play. Jay Hoffman, assistant coach of the 1999 U.S. women's World Cup team, demonstrates how teams can exploit an opponent's flanks to penetrate and get behind the defense. Effective flank play has become even more important in recent years due to the improved organization and sophistication of modern defenses.

In chapter 8 Steve Locker of Harvard University examines a strategy that has gained greater recognition and acceptance in recent years—predetermined patterns of team play. In this scenario players follow patterns of movement that provide the greatest opportunity for penetrating an opponent's defense. Teams constantly adjust patterns as the ball changes location to take best advantage of the situation. Patterned play is a team concept in every sense of the word because each player fulfills a specific role within a given pattern.

CHAPTER 4

Possession Soccer

Dean Foti
Syracuse University

Theoretically, to score goals a team must have possession of the ball. Consequently, the more possession a team has, the greater its opportunity to create scoring chances. To take it a step further, the more scoring chances a team has, the more likely it is to score goals.

The term *possession soccer* refers to the ability of a group of players to maintain possession of the ball during play against a live opponent. In a full-field 11-a-side game, possession play can range from methodically building out of the back and playing through thirds of the field to playing directly by driving longer balls into the opponent's half of the field to be won or repossessed and maintained to create scoring opportunities. To maintain possession with the purpose of creating scoring opportunities, a team must find a balance between deliberate building play and more direct penetrating play.

As a style of play, possession soccer yields several benefits over a 90-minute game. First, a team that is good at maintaining possession will be able to regulate the tempo of the game. While establishing its own rhythm of play, it in effect takes its opponent out of theirs. Second, the team that has more possession play can dictate the tactical direction of the game. The ability of a team to carry out any game plan, whether it be exploiting an opponent's defensive weakness or emphasizing its attacking strengths, depends on having the ball. Superior possession play allows a team to determine tactically what will take place on the field. Third, a team that excels at keeping possession of the ball will eventually wear down an opponent, both physically and mentally. Defending and chasing the ball for 90 minutes is physically taxing and psychologically disconcerting. All these factors take their toll and aid in breaking down an opponent.

But the most important benefit of possession soccer is that the team with more possession will have the opportunity to create more scoring chances. Having said this, I must point out that keeping possession only to control the ball will not create scoring opportunities. Possession for possession's sake will not produce goals, but possession play with a purpose will. Possession play to find numerical advantages throughout the field, to penetrate and unbalance an opponent's defense, is what will break down defenses, create scoring opportunities, and produce goals.

Several basic building blocks are prerequisites for effective possession soccer. First, players must be able to make correct decisions quickly during play. Second, individual team members must have a common understanding about when to keep possession of the ball and when to go forward and penetrate. Last, when concise decision making and a clear understanding of the possession vs. penetration concept are in place, a team can focus on increasing the speed of play, on moving the ball quickly within the team to unbalance the opponent's defense. Slow play allows the defense time to react comfortably to every movement of the ball. Each time a player in possession of the ball pauses to decide what to do next the defense has time to adjust.

If a team can increase speed of play by acting quickly on decisions and thus moving the ball rapidly from player to player, the defense has less time to react and keep up. By not allowing the defense time to provide adequate pressure, cover, and balance, opportunities to penetrate will arise.

The following exercises are designed to improve possession play. They are aimed at developing and improving the basic building blocks of possession soccer while recognizing that the objective is to penetrate and create scoring opportunities to increase goal production.

23 3 vs. 1 in a Grid

Purpose

To improve ability to keep possession of the ball; to identify the proper angles of support by the players without the ball; and to identify when the players without the ball should arrive in these supporting positions.

Organization

Three attacking players take positions within the perimeter of a 12-by-12-yard grid. One defender is in the middle of the grid.

Procedure

1. The three attacking players pass among themselves and try to maintain possession of the ball.

2. The live defender in the middle tries to touch the ball, intercept a pass, or force an attacking player into making an errant pass out of the grid.

3. The defender who successfully disrupts play switches roles with the attacking player who was responsible for the loss of possession.

Key Points

- Players without the ball must move within the perimeter to create good angles so the player in possession can find them with a pass.

- Players without the ball must arrive in these good supporting positions early (while the ball is en route) to allow the player in possession to pass quickly before being closed down or tackled by the lone defender.

- The player with the ball must pass and move, rather than just pass and stand, to create a good angle to get the ball back.

- Stress proper weight of passes, proper location of passes, and proper body position when receiving a pass (hips open to the game and in a position to see the whole field).

continued

Variations

- Limit the number of touches by the three attacking players (permitting fewer touches makes it more challenging to keep possession).

- Adjust the size of the grid (a smaller grid makes it more challenging to keep possession; a larger one makes it easier).

- Identify a certain number of passes as a goal (for example, making 10 consecutive passes equals a goal).

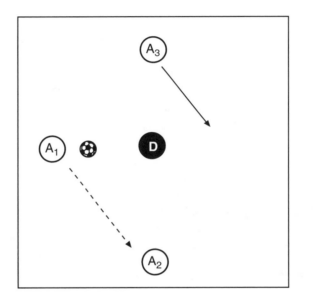

Drill 23

---

24 4 vs. 2 in a Grid

Purpose

To improve ability to keep possession of the ball and to identify proper angles and timing of support.

Organization

Four attacking players take positions within the perimeter of a 15-by-15-yard grid. Two defenders are in the middle of the grid.

Procedure

1. The four attacking players pass among themselves and try to maintain possession of the ball.

2. The two live defenders in the middle try to intercept a pass or force an attacking player into making an errant pass out of the grid.

3. When the attacking players lose possession, the defender who has been in the middle the longest switches with the attacking player who caused the loss of possession.

Key Points

- Emphasize the key points in 3 vs. 1.

- Players should move the ball quickly from player to player to unbalance the two defenders, that is, get them "square." Until the attacking players can unbalance the

continued

defenders, their objective should be to keep possession of the ball and move it quickly. When the attackers pull the defenders out of proper defensive position, their goal is to penetrate, to split the defenders.

- Holding the ball allows the defenders time to adjust; moving it quickly will unbalance them and open up opportunities to penetrate.

- Emphasize the importance of recognizing when to keep possession vs. when to penetrate.

Variations

- Limit the number of touches by the four attacking players to get the ball moving more quickly between them.

- Adjust the size of the grid (smaller to make it more challenging, larger to make it easier to keep possession).

- Add a fifth attacking player (to make it 5 vs. 2) so that keeping possession is easier.

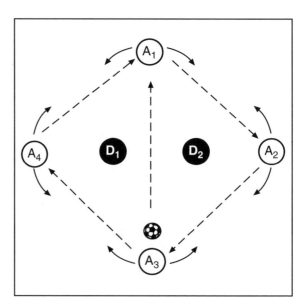

- To add an element of transition, require the defenders, at the instant they win the ball, to complete a pass before getting out of the middle. The attacking players can step in to prevent the defenders from completing a pass. If the attacking players win the ball back, they open back up and keep possession. The game continues until the two defenders can win the ball and complete a pass between themselves.

- Identify a certain number of passes as a goal (for example, making 10 consecutive passes equals a goal).

Drill 24

25   6 vs. 3 in a Grid

Purpose

To improve possession play, speed of play, and transition play.

Organization

Three groups of three players (A_R, A_G, and D_B), each group with a different color, take positions within the perimeter of a 15-by-30-yard grid.

Procedure

1. The attacking team will always have six players (two groups of three). They will pass among themselves and try to maintain possession of the ball within the grid.

2. The remaining three players are live defenders. They will try to close down the attacking team and intercept a pass.

continued

3. When the defenders win possession of the ball, the trio of attacking players responsible for the loss of possession immediately becomes the defending trio. The original trio of defenders then teams up with the remaining trio to form a new team of six attacking players.

4. The game is continuous with no pauses to switch roles. With each loss of possession a new trio defends and the other two trios team up to try to keep possession of the ball.

Key Points

- Players on the attacking team must support the player with the ball early and at good supporting angles. They will have to interchange and move, both to the center of the grid to provide penetrating supporting angles and to the perimeter to provide supporting options.

- Emphasize quick ball movement within the team in possession of the ball. With each change in possession, emphasize quick transition from attack to defense and vice versa. Always work to increase speed of play.

- Emphasize drawing the defense to one end of the grid through quick possession play and then identifying when and how to change the point of the attack to the other side of the grid.

- Emphasize the importance of recognizing when to keep possession vs. when to penetrate or change the point of the attack.

Variations

- Limit the number of touches by the attacking team (for example, limit the attacking team to two touches).

- Adjust the size of the grid.

- Limit the number of touches by each colored trio of players (for example, reds have one touch, blues have two touches, and greens have unlimited touches).

- Add a neutral player who is always on the team with the ball (that is, make it 7 vs. 3).

- Identify a certain number of passes as a goal (for example, making 10 consecutive passes equals a goal).

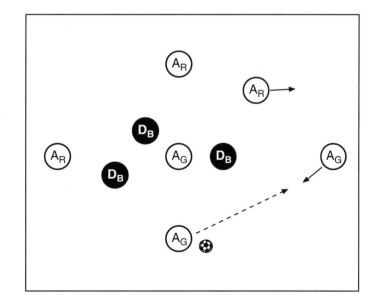

Drill 25

26 4 vs. 4 + 2 in a Grid

Purpose

To improve possession play, speed of play, and transition play.

Organization

Two teams of four with two neutral players take positions within a 20-by-40-yard grid.

Procedure

1. One team of four and the two neutral players pass among themselves and try to maintain possession of the ball. The remaining four players are live defenders (that is, 6 vs. 4)

2. If the defenders intercept a pass, they then team with the two neutral players and try to maintain possession of the ball. The other team of four immediately becomes the defending team.

3. The two neutral players are always on the team with the ball.

4. The game is continuous with no pauses to switch roles.

Key Points

- Players must provide early support at good supporting angles.
- Attempt to increase speed of play.
- The teams should be quick in transition from attack to defense and vice versa.
- Players should learn to make good decisions about when to keep possession vs. when to penetrate or change the point of the attack.

Variations

- Limit the number of touches by the attacking team.
- Limit the number of touches by the neutral players only.
- Vary the number of touches within the attacking team (for example, the attacking team of four has two touches and the neutral players have one touch).
- Each time a neutral player receives the ball he or she must play it to the other neutral player before distributing it to the team in possession.
- Identify a certain number of passes as a goal (for example, making 10 passes equals a goal).
- Adjust the size of the grid.

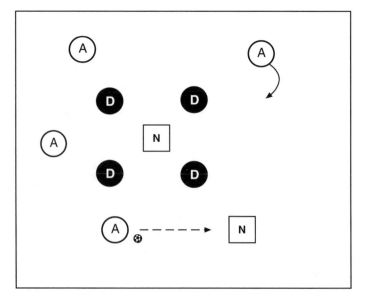

27 Cone Game

Purpose

To improve possession play and speed of play.

Organization

Three teams of six (A_R, A_G, and D_B), each with a different color scrimmage vest, take positions within a 40-by-60-yard field.

Procedure

1. Two teams of six combine to form the attacking team. They pass among themselves and try to maintain possession of the ball (that is, 12 vs. 6).

2. The remaining six are live defenders who try to intercept a pass. Each of the six players holds a cone (or perhaps a different color scrimmage vest) in his or her hand.

3. When the six defenders win possession of the ball they immediately drop the cones. The team responsible for the loss of possession immediately becomes the new defending team. Each member of the new defending team must immediately pick up a cone. They may not begin trying to win the ball back until each member has picked up a cone.

4. The original defending team then joins the remaining six to form the new attacking team.

5. The game is continuous. When a team loses possession, the new attacking team immediately puts the ball in play (while the members of the new defending team are picking up cones) and quickly tries to string together consecutive passes.

Key Points

- Players should provide early support at good supporting angles.
- Attempt to increase speed of play.
- Players should make quick transitions from attack to defense and vice versa.
- Players should learn to make good decisions about when to keep possession vs. when to penetrate or change the point of attack.

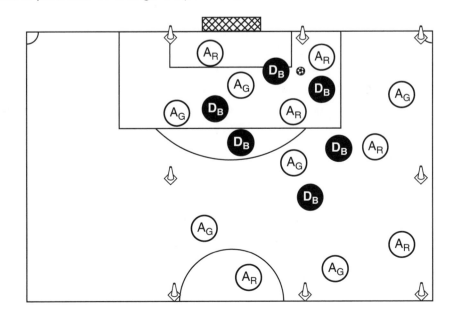

continued

Variations

- Adjust the team sizes (for example, 7 vs. 7 vs. 7, 8 vs. 8 vs. 8).
- Adjust the size of the field.
- Limit the number of touches by one, two, or all three groups of six players.
- Identify a certain number of passes as a goal (for example, making 10 passes equals a goal).

Drill 27

28 100 Passes

Purpose

To improve possession play.

Organization

Two teams of eight and one neutral player take positions within a 40-by-60-yard field.

Procedure

1. One team of eight and the neutral player pass among themselves and try to maintain possession of the ball. The remaining eight are live defenders (that is, 9 vs. 8).
2. If the defenders intercept a pass they then team with the neutral player to maintain possession of the ball. The other team of eight immediately becomes the defending team.
3. The neutral player is always on the team with the ball.
4. The game is continuous with no pauses to switch roles.
5. The object is to be the first team to reach 100 passes, though these need not occur in one possession. A team that in its first possession passes the ball consecutively six times before losing it will pick up the count at seven when they win the ball back. The game continues until one team reaches 100 passes.

Key Points

- Players must provide early support at good supporting angles.
- Attempt to increase speed of play.
- Players should be quick in transition from attack to defense and vice versa.
- Players should learn to make good decisions about when to keep possession vs. when to penetrate or change the point of the attack.

Variations

- Adjust the team sizes (6 vs. 6 + 1, 7 vs. 7 + 1, 9 vs. 9 + 1).
- Adjust the size of the field.
- Add another neutral player (that is, 8 vs. 8 + 2).
- Limit the touches of the attacking team or the neutral player, or vary it for each of them.

continued

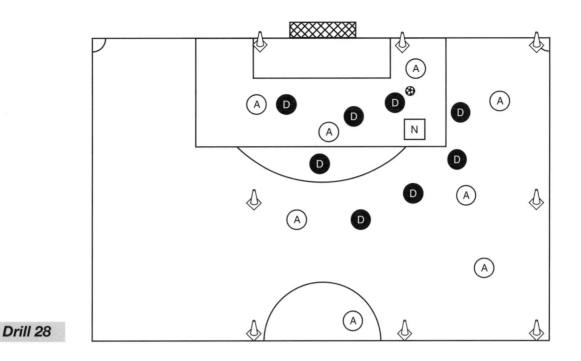

Drill 28

29 Consecutive Passes

Purpose

To improve possession play.

Organization

Two teams of eight take positions within a 40-by-60-yard field.

Procedure

1. One team of eight pass among themselves and try to maintain possession of the ball. The remaining eight are live defenders (that is, 8 vs. 8).

2. The team in possession of the ball tries to string together as many consecutive passes as possible each time it has possession of the ball (that is, the first possession may total six passes, the second four passes, the third 10 passes).

3. Specify a time (8, 10, or 12 minutes) as the length of the game.

4. At the end of the period, the team that has strung together the most consecutive passes in a single possession wins (that is, if team A's best possession consisted of 15 consecutive passes and team D's best possession consisted of 18, team D wins).

5. Designate a player to be the counter for each team.

Key Points

- Players must provide early support at good supporting angles.
- Attempt to increase speed of play.
- Players should be quick in transition from attack to defense and vice versa.
- Players should learn to make good decisions about when to keep possession vs. when to penetrate or change the point of attack.

continued

Variations

- Adjust the team sizes (to 5 vs. 5, 6 vs. 6, or 9 vs. 9).
- Adjust the size of the field.
- Add a neutral player or two.
- Limit the number of touches by the attacking team or the neutral player, or vary it for each of them.
- Split your team into four teams and have a round-robin tournament (have four teams of six play eight-minute games).

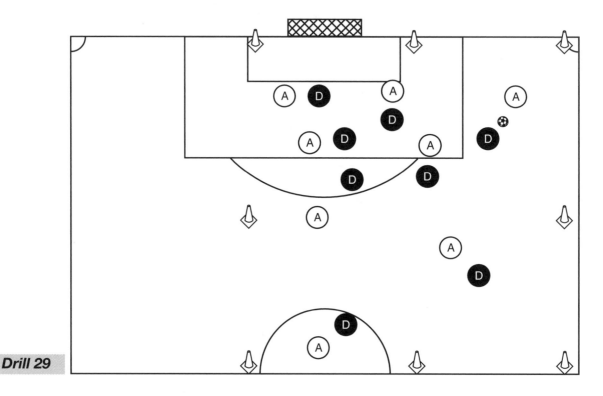

Drill 29

30 Lose It and Sit

Purpose

To improve possession play.

Organization

Two teams of eight with two neutral players take positions within a 40-by-60-yard field.

Procedure

1. One team of eight and the two neutral players pass among themselves and try to maintain possession of the ball. The remaining eight players are live defenders (that is, 10 vs. 8).

2. If the defenders intercept a pass, they then team with the neutral players to maintain possession of the ball. The other team of eight now becomes the defending team.

continued

3. Every time a team loses possession, the player responsible for losing it (excluding the neutral players) must come off and wait on the side of the field (the coach can identify the guilty party). Team size will fluctuate with each loss of possession.

4. Identify a certain number of passes as a goal (for example, making 10 passes equals a goal). Each time a team scores a goal it may reinstate a waiting player back into the game.

5. Specify a time (10, 12, or 15 minutes) as the length of the game.

6. At the conclusion of the designated time the team with the most players on the field (not including neutral players) wins.

Key Points

- Players must provide early support at good supporting angles.
- Attempt to increase speed of play.
- Teams should be quick in transition from attack to defense and vice versa.
- Players should learn to make good decisions about when to keep possession vs. when to penetrate or change the point of attack.

Variations

- Limit the number of touches by the attacking team.
- Limit the number of touches by the neutral players.
- Vary the number of touches within the attacking team (for example, attacking players have two touches and neutral players have one touch).
- Adjust the size of the field.
- Vary the number of neutral players.

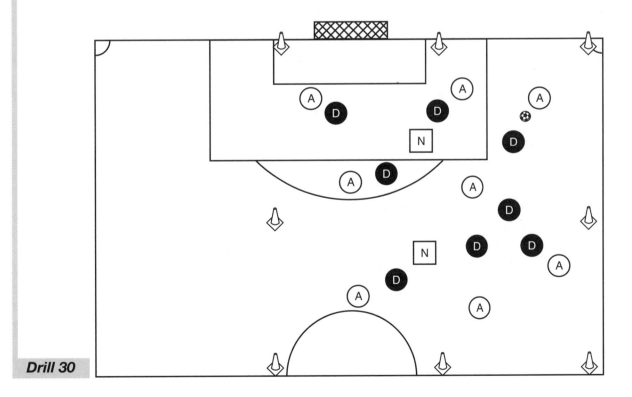

Drill 30

31 Possession to Targets

Purpose

To improve possession play.

Organization

Two teams of eight plus one neutral player take positions within a 44-by-70-yard field. Two additional neutral target players take positions at each end of the playing field just beyond the end lines.

Procedure

1. One team of eight and the three neutral players (one within the game itself and one on each end line) pass among themselves and try to maintain possession of the ball. The remaining eight players are live defenders (that is, 11 vs. 8).

2. If the defenders intercept a pass, they then team with the neutral players to maintain possession of the ball. The other team of eight becomes the defending team.

3. The neutral players are always on the team with the ball. The neutral players on the end lines move horizontally and act as target players when they are ahead of the ball and as supporting players when they are behind the ball.

4. The team with the ball keeps possession until it is appropriate to find a neutral player on either end line. The neutral player then has one touch to play it back into the team that played it to him or her.

5. The object is to keep possession until it is appropriate to penetrate or change the point of attack by finding the neutral player on the end line that is farthest away.

Key Points

- Emphasize the key points in previous possession games.
- Players should identify the appropriate time to change the point of attack.
- Emphasize drawing the defense to one end of the field before changing the point of attack.
- Emphasize supporting the neutral target players early (while the ball is en route to them) because they only have one touch to put the ball back into play.

Variations

- Limit the number of touches by the attacking team.
- Vary the number of touches by the neutral player within the game.
- Vary the number of touches by the neutral players on the end lines.
- Restrict the neutral players on the end lines from playing a ball to the neutral player within the game.
- Restrict the neutral players on the end lines from playing a ball back to the player who played it into them.
- Designate the neutral player within the game as a free player (a player who cannot be defended) and require him or her to find the neutral player farthest away each time he or she receives the ball.
- Specify a certain number of consecutive passes as a goal.

continued

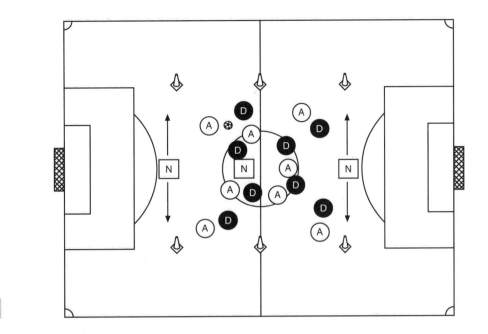

Drill 31

32 Replace the Target Player

Purpose

To improve possession play.

Organization

Two teams of 10 (eight players within the field of play and a target player at each end line) and a neutral player take positions within a 40-by-60-yard field.

Procedure

1. One team of 10 and the neutral player pass among themselves and try to maintain possession of the ball. The remaining 10 players are live defenders (that is, 11 vs. 10).

2. If the defenders intercept a pass, they then team with the neutral player to maintain possession of the ball. The other team of 10 becomes the defending team.

3. The neutral player within the field of play is always on the team with the ball but cannot pass to, or receive balls from, the end-line players.

4. The target players on each end line may move horizontally to support the play.

5. The object is to keep possession of the ball. The twist in this drill is that when a player passes the ball to the teammate on the end line, he or she must go to the end line and take that player's place as the new target. The original target player has one touch to play the ball back into his or her teammates and then go onto the field of play to join them in keeping possession of the ball.

6. The end-line players are prohibited from playing back into the neutral player (they must find a teammate). They are not permitted to defend each other on the end line.

Key Point

Emphasize the key points in the Possession to Targets exercise.

continued

Variations

- Limit the number of touches by the attacking team.
- Vary the number of touches by the neutral player within the game.
- Vary the number of touches by the end-line target players.
- Identify a certain number of passes as a goal (for example, making 10 passes equals a goal).

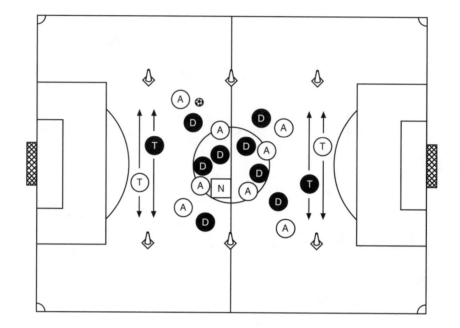

Drill 32

33 Three-Goal Game

Purpose

To improve possession play.

Organization

Two teams of eight plus two neutral players take positions within half of a field. Set up three small goals across each end line with cones.

Procedure

1. One team of eight and two neutral players pass among themselves and try to maintain possession of the ball. The remaining eight players are live defenders (that is, 10 vs. 8).

2. If the defenders intercept a pass, they then team with the two neutral players to maintain possession of the ball. The other team of eight now becomes the defending team.

3. The two neutral players are always on the team with the ball and are allowed to score.

4. The object is for a team to keep possession of the ball until it can find a numerical advantage and penetrate.

5. A goal is scored by a player dribbling through any of the three goals (cones) uncontested.

6. Each team is responsible for defending three goals and attacking the opposite three.

continued

Key Points

- Emphasize the key points in the previous possession games.
- Emphasize the importance of recognizing when to keep possession vs. when to penetrate or change the point of attack.
- Teams should attempt to increase speed of play to unbalance the defense.
- If it is not appropriate to penetrate, the team should maintain patience and discipline to keep possession until it can find a numerical advantage (that is, the team should learn not to force it).

Variations

- Limit the number of touches by the neutral players.
- Vary the number of neutral players.
- Require that a certain number of passes be completed before a team can go to goal (for example, a team must complete 10 passes before it can attack the goal).
- Establish a halfway line and require that all players on the attacking team be up to the line before they can score a goal. In addition, vary the number of touches allowed per player in each half of the field. For example, in the back half permit two touches; in the attacking half allow unlimited touches.

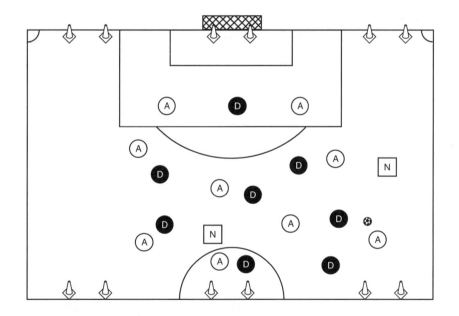

Drill 33

34 Big Goal—Small Goal

Purpose

To improve possession play.

Organization

Arrange two teams of eight and one neutral player in positions similar to a full-sided game. Use half of a field. Three small goals are on the midfield line; one large goal (with goalkeeper) is on the end line.

continued

Procedure

1. One team of eight plus the neutral player pass among themselves and try to maintain possession of the ball. The remaining eight players are live defenders (that is, 9 vs. 8 + goalkeeper).

2. If the defenders win the ball, they then team up with the neutral player to keep possession. The other team of eight becomes the defending team.

3. The teams of eight take positions as in an 11-a-side game.

4. The team defending the large goal attacks the three small goals and scores by dribbling through the cones uncontested.

5. The team defending the three small goals attacks the big goal and must shoot for goal and beat the goalkeeper as in a normal 11-a-side game.

6. The object for each team is to keep possession until it can find a numerical advantage, penetrate, and score a goal.

Key Points

- Emphasize the key points listed for the Three-Goal Game.

- Emphasize these points when scoring chances arise in attacking the big goal—beat the goalkeeper, finish knock downs and all chances, and score goals.

Variations

- Use the variations offered for the Three-Goal Game.

- Have the teams switch sides so each gets to attack the big goal.

- Replace the three small goals with two big goals (one on each flank on the midfield line).

- Replace the three small goals with one big goal in the center. Now it's a game with regular-size goals.

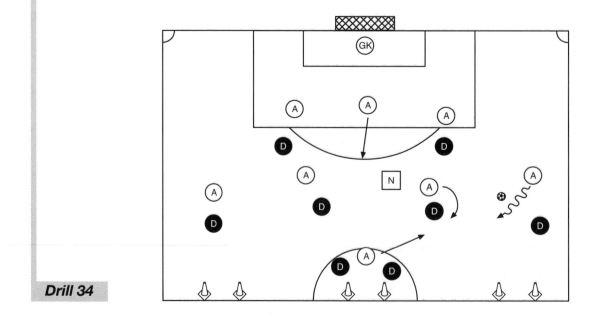

Drill 34

CHAPTER 5

Changing the Point of Attack

Ronald W. Quinn

Xavier University

Soccer is a rhythmic activity. The play ebbs and flows as players move the ball to score goals or position themselves to deny goals. Goals can occur in almost limitless ways—in countless player combinations in areas of the field where players can exploit spaces in the defense to create scoring opportunities. Successful attacks, however, usually result from the ability of a team to create sufficient space in the final third and more specifically in the immediate area of the goal. How a team achieves this territorial advantage is the focus of this book. One method a team employs to penetrate and get behind an opponent's defense is to change the point of attack.

Conceptually the game is played within a set of general and specific principles. General playing principles include time and space relationships along with technical, physical, psychological, and tactical understanding of each player. Specific attacking principles include penetration, depth and width, mobility, and improvisation. Principles of defending play include immediate chase, delay, concentration, control and restraint, and balance. We need to look, too, at how players use these specific principles as individuals, in small groups, and as a team. The manner in which players within a team apply these general and specific principles will depend on their ability.

The game of soccer has also been described as a series of small-group tactics and player movements tied together by changes in the point of attack. This chapter provides a series of activities that a team can use to achieve field penetration through changing the point of attack. The purpose of this particular playing pattern is tied to the checks and balances within the principles of play. If a team is trying to create space, its opponent is attempting to deny it through immediate pressure, compactness, and balance in defense. Thus, if a team is compact defensively and attempting to gain a numerical advantage in the immediate area of the ball, then the attacking team might make a tactical choice to widen the defense and play the ball to an area with fewer defenders. The attacking team can accomplish this by establishing a passing pattern that changes the point of attack.

When designing a practice session for changing the point of attack or considering the extent to which a team should employ this tactic, the coach should examine the ability of the team's players. Players need to be able to serve the ball quickly and accurately at least 30 yards, possess the field vision to see players at a distance, and be able to create space behind the defense or on the flank.

This practice session helps players understand why, when, and how to exploit spaces in the defense by changing the point of attack. The activities move from simple warm-up movements with clear objectives to more complex activities in which players will need to select the correct decision from several alternatives. Time for each activity can range from a few minutes to 20 minutes or more depending on the success and motivational level of the players. Success in changing the point of attack will rely on the patience and technical ability of each player to hold the ball, the ability of each player to take pressure off the ball in preparation for a service, and the ability of players off the ball to recognize when to move into passing lanes to receive balls.

35   Interpassing With Four Players

Purpose

To begin preparing players for practice through small-group interaction.

Organization

In an area approximately 20 by 30 yards, organize groups of four players, each group with a ball.

Procedure

1. Within the suggested area or larger, depending on the number of groups, players interpass while avoiding the other groups. Groups of four focus only on partners while ignoring the movements of other groups.

2. Play for two minutes, then stop, group, and stretch for two to three minutes. Repeat the passing pattern and perform a second stretch.

Key Points

• While passing, teammates should keep the other three players in full view, thereby expanding their field vision. The player with the ball should never have to look for a teammate to pass to.

• Emphasize making eye contact and giving each other oral cues.

Variation

Give one or two players a one-touch condition. The other two or three are playmakers, allowed unlimited touches.

Drill 35

36 Short-Short-Long

Purpose

To introduce the concept of switching the ball or changing the point of attack. This creates a rhythm of playing close support, thus relieving pressure on the ball to allow a longer service to a free player.

Organization

Arrange groups of four players with one ball per group in one-quarter to one-half of the field. No opponent applies pressure this time.

Procedure

1. Players play two short, or supporting, passes and then a longer pass of 20 to 30 yards to the third teammate.

2. Another short-short-long sequence follows immediately. Encourage players to play a one-touch pass to a close supporting player following the long pass.

Key Points

- Allow players enough time to get into a playing rhythm.
- Encourage players to play with the same intensity and concentration as they do in a real match.
- Stress various types of services—chips or instep drives.
- Players should play balls to feet.

Variations

As with all activities, you can make the activity more complex by having several groups share the same space, limiting the number of touches, or adding pressure from an opponent.

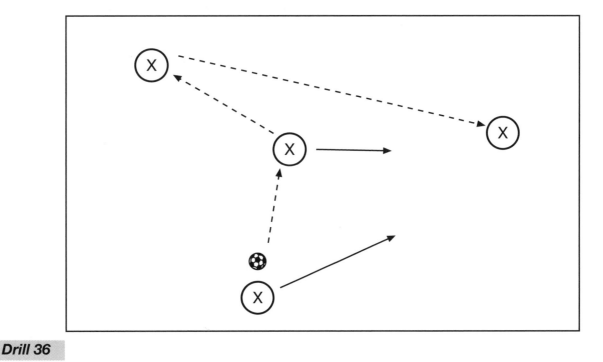

Drill 36

37 In the Zone

Purpose

To change the point of attack to penetrate defenses.

Organization

Organize two teams of eight players, placed in four alternating zones. The field is 30 by 40 yards; each zone is 30 by 10 yards. Place one team in zones 1 and 3 and the other in zones 2 and 4.

Procedure

1. Teams pass the ball until they create a penetration pass through their opponent's zone, playing the ball through to their team in the other zone.

2. If the defending team intercepts the ball, they look to play to their teammates in the corresponding zone. Zones 2 and 3 will always be the middle zones.

3. A team scores a point each time they successfully play through an opponent's zone. Change zones so that players in the end zones have an opportunity to be in the middle.

Key Points

- Patience and looking forward first after each pass is the first priority.

- Playing a penetrating pass should be the players' first option. If that is not available, players should change the angle and direction of the pass to find a new open channel.

Variations

- Restrict players to a limited number of touches.

- Permit one player from an end zone to move into the opponent's zone, creating a 4 vs. 1 environment.

- Permit two players from an end zone to move into the opponent's zone, creating a 4 vs. 2 environment. You may need to increase zone sizes for this activity.

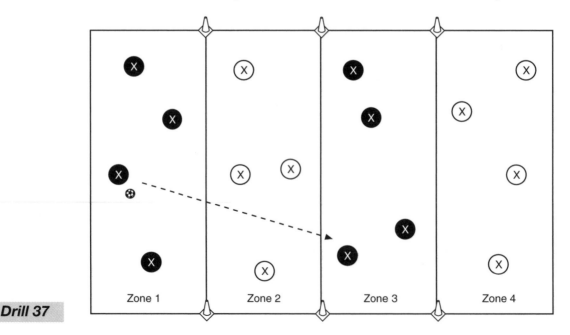

Drill 37

38 Group 4 vs. 2

Purpose

To establish a passing tendency in which changing the point of attack is followed by supporting runs.

Organization

Position three or more groups of six players in 10-by-15-yard grids. Grids should be 30 to 40 yards apart in a triangle fashion. Players set up for a 4 vs. 2 in each grid with one ball per grid. Each player has a permanent partner throughout the exercise.

Procedure

1. Each group plays 4 vs. 2 possession. On the coach's signal the player with the ball serves it to another grid. (Prearrange which grids are passing to each other.)

2. The player who serves the ball and his or her partner sprint into the grid to which the ball was sent. These two new players become the two players in the middle.

3. Four vs. two play continues until the coach gives the next signal to serve the ball.

Key Points

• Players must not hesitate before sprinting to the next grid when the server plays the ball.

• Receiving players must be alert and ready to receive a ball from another grid.

• Players receiving the ball immediately begin passing to maintain their passing rhythm.

Variations

• Play one-touch or two-touch passing.

• Identify the type of service given in the long pass to the next grid.

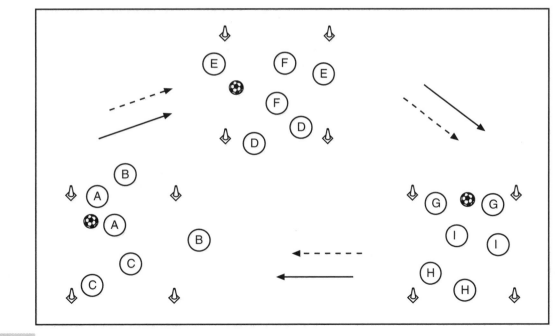

Drill 38

39 Dynamic 4 vs. 2 + 2

Purpose

To encourage changing the point of attack immediately upon winning the ball.

Organization

Organize two groups of four players with one ball. Set up two grids or areas for players to play 4 vs. 2, leaving the other two players in the second grid. Grids should be 20 to 30 yards apart.

Procedure

1. The group plays 4 vs. 2 in the designated area (grid A) with the other two players in the second grid (grid B).

2. When the two defending players win the ball they immediately play to teammates in opposing grids and run to support them.

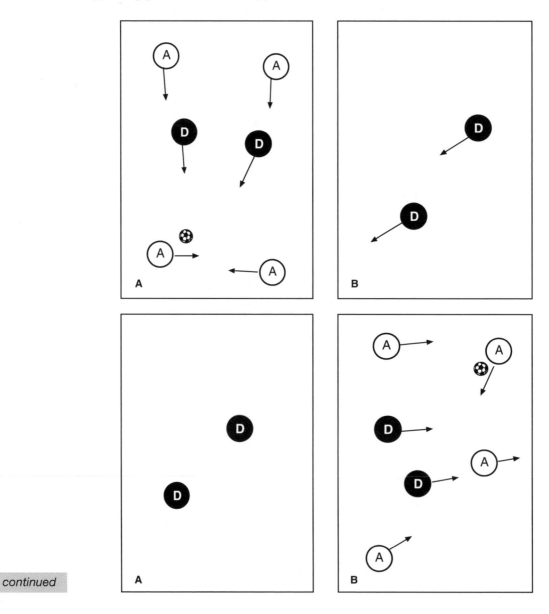

continued

3. At the same time the player who lost the ball and his or her partner run to the grid to become the new defenders. Roles reverse, and the two remaining players continue moving in readiness for teammates to win the ball back.

4. Play for two- to three-minute intervals. The team in possession of the ball at the end of the period wins the round. Award points or apply consequences such as sit-ups, push-ups, or short sprints to create a more competitive environment.

Key Points

- Fitness activities that you add as a consequence should be reasonable so that players can complete the task quickly and restart the activity. Give players 5 or 10 reps of a task, not 50.

- The two players in grid A must support each other to take pressure off the ball in preparation for a service to change the point of attack.

- Upon winning the ball the two players in the opposing grid should be moving to receive the pass early.

- The two new defending players should move quickly to put pressure on the ball in the new grid.

Variation

To make the activity more complex, allow one of the two players in grid B to join teammates in grid A, making it a 4 vs. 3 environment. When the three win the ball, they play it to the single long player. All players then run to the new space except one from the new defending team who stays behind as the long target.

Drill 39

40 Team Knockout I

Purpose

To encourage group communication, support, ball possession, and changing the point of attack. This activity and the next two create situations in which players are in small-group or team environments. Application of environmental conditions will emphasize certain playing tendencies.

Organization

Arrange two teams of at least eight players on half a field.

Procedure

1. Team A is on the field, each player with a ball. Team D, without balls, stands anywhere along the sideline.

2. On the signal, team D runs onto the field and attempts to kick all the balls off the field. The coach starts the clock on the signal and stops it when the last ball is kicked off the field.

3. Team A members who have had their ball kicked off the field should help other team A members by getting into positions where they can receive passes. Remember, time does not stop until team D kicks all the balls off the field.

4. After the last ball is played out, reverse team roles. Team D tries to kick out all the balls quicker than team A.

continued

Key Point

This game follows a logical progression from 1 vs. 1 to 8 vs. 8 with one team attempting to keep possession on half a field or playing an indirect style while the other team is exerting an all-out effort to dispossess their opponents.

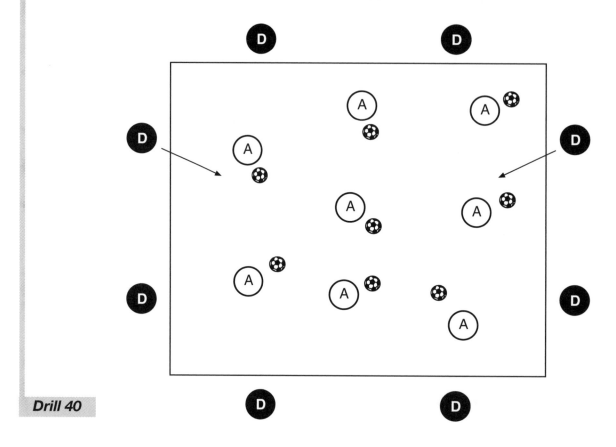

Drill 40

---

41 Team Knockout II

Purpose

To dribble to relieve pressure and change the point of attack.

Procedure

This activity is the same as Team Knockout I except that team D players must now win the ball and immediately dribble the ball across a touch line or end line before a team A member can win the ball back. When team D gets all the balls across the line, the coach stops the clock.

Key Point

The difference now is that players on both teams apply immediate pressure upon losing the ball. Team A still tries to maintain possession, and team D attempts to win a ball and immediately change direction and sprint to an open area.

continued

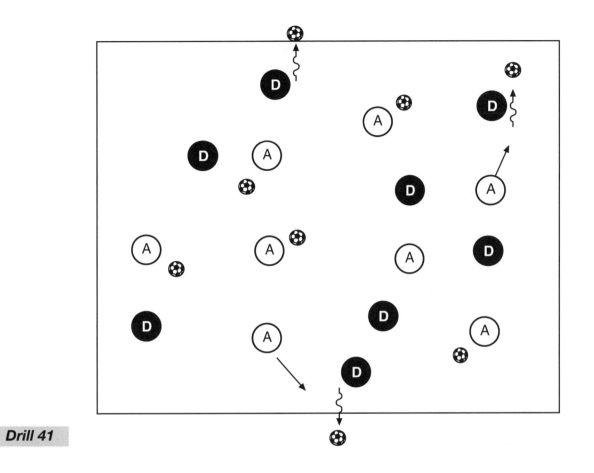

Drill 41

42 Team Knockout III

Purpose

To pass to relieve pressure and change the point of attack.

Procedure

1. This activity is the same as Team Knockout I and II except that only half (four) of the players from team D run onto the field, creating an 8 vs. 4 environment.

2. When team D players win the ball, they must pass the ball to the feet of a teammate who is along one of the lines.

3. When team D passes all the balls across the line the coach stops the clock.

Key Points

- Both teams continue to apply immediate pressure upon losing the ball. Team D, however, now must win the ball and immediately change direction to get the ball wide and outside to target players.

- This activity will take four rounds for every player to play each role.

- Balls kicked out with no clear possession from either team receive no points. The coach may decrease team A's time by a certain amount for each ball that team D played to the feet of outside target players.

continued

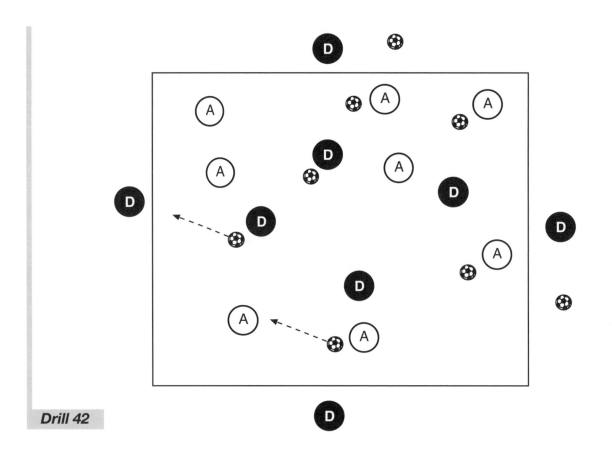

Drill 42

43 Team Knockout IV (to Large Goal)

Purpose

To introduce a direct style of play when changing the point of attack. In this version defending players win balls and attack a large goal.

Procedure

1. This activity is the same as Team Knockout I, II, and III except that when team D players win the ball, they attack a large goal.

2. When team D scores all the balls or balls are played out of bounds from missed shots, the coach stops the clock. Balls played over a touch line may be played in as in a regular match.

Key Points

- Both teams continue to apply immediate pressure upon losing the ball. Team D, however, now must win the ball and immediately change direction and attack the goal.

- Balls that are kicked out with no clear possession from either team receive no points. The coach may reduce team A's time by a certain amount for each score by team D. Use goalkeepers who can be neutral and keep score within their games.

continued

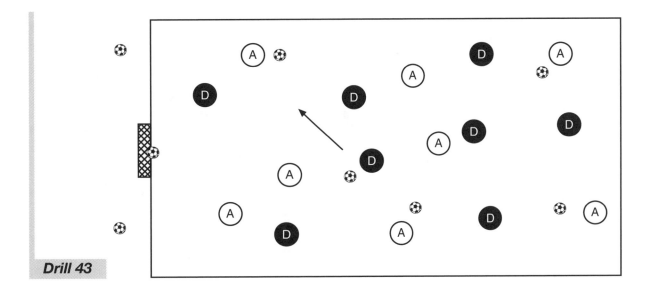

Drill 43

44 Put Down—Pick Up

Purpose

To be the first team to hit all targets by changing the point of attack.

Organization

Position three teams of six, in different colored vests, on half a field. Players on one of the teams will be targets. Space them evenly throughout the field in circles with a five-yard radius, preferably near the sides of the field but not off it.

Procedure

1. Each team wears vests of different colors—red, yellow, and blue. Teams red and yellow play 6 vs. 6 with one ball, attempting to get the ball to the blue target team.

2. Players on team blue hold a green vest and a cone. The object is for the red and yellow teams to play the ball to all six targets.

3. Targets must stay within their five-yard-radius circles. When a red team member plays a ball to a blue target, the blue player puts down his or her cone. The red team wins when all blue target players have dropped their cones.

4. However, if the yellow team plays a ball to a blue target, that player drops his or her green vest. If a cone was already down, the target player picks up the cone and puts down the vest. The target player cannot have both objects on the ground at the same time. The first team to get all their objects on the ground wins the round.

Key Points

- Rotate team roles until every team has played each other.
- Focus on early play to targets. Defending teams may not enter the target circles.

continued

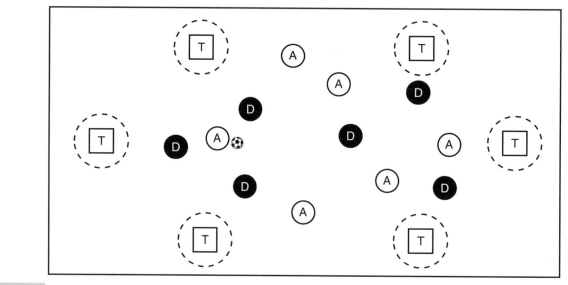

Drill 44

45 Checkers

Purpose

To score goals by changing the point of attack while playing through designated grids.

Organization

Arrange two teams of eight on a field either 40 by 50 yards or 40 by 60 yards with two large goals. The field should be marked in 10-by-10-yard grids.

Procedure

Teams play 8 vs. 8 to the large goals (with goalkeepers) with the following conditions:

1. A team cannot have more than one player in a grid.

2. Teams cannot pass the ball through more than two similar grids—that is, two vertical, two horizontal, or two diagonal grids—without changing the direction of the ball. For example, a ball played horizontally from a grid can be played once more horizontally before it must be played diagonally or vertically.

Key Points

- Passing violations result in loss of possession.
- Look to expand players' vision to find open grids.

Variations

- Limit the number of touches.
- To extend passing length, do not permit players to play balls to adjacent horizontal or vertical grids. A diagonal pass to an adjacent grid is permitted if followed by a two-grid horizontal or vertical pass.
- Take all conditions off in the last row of grids in front of each goal.

continued

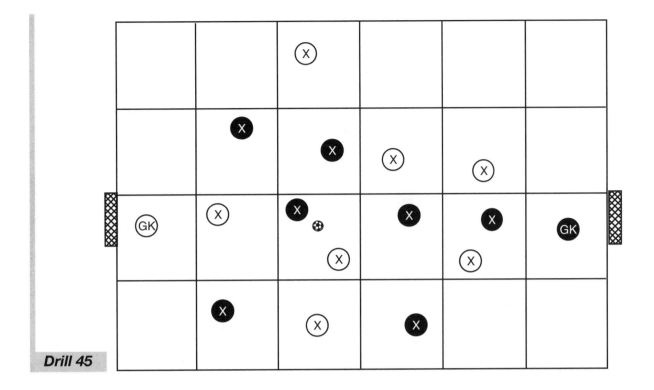

Drill 45

46 Going Vertical

Purpose

To change the point of attack through diagonal passing.

Organization

Organize two teams of 8 to 11 players. Play to two large goals on a full or three-quarter-length field. Divide the field into five vertical zones.

Procedure

Teams play to the large goals (with goalkeepers) with the following conditions:

1. Every pass must be played to a different vertical zone.

2. Dribbling is permitted within a zone.

3. When a transition occurs, the ball must be played into another zone.

Key Points

- Emphasize quick diagonal passing using the entire width of the field while moving forward.

- Encourage finishing with a one-touch shot from a cross or diagonal pass.

- Instruct players to come diagonally off a defender to receive a pass.

continued

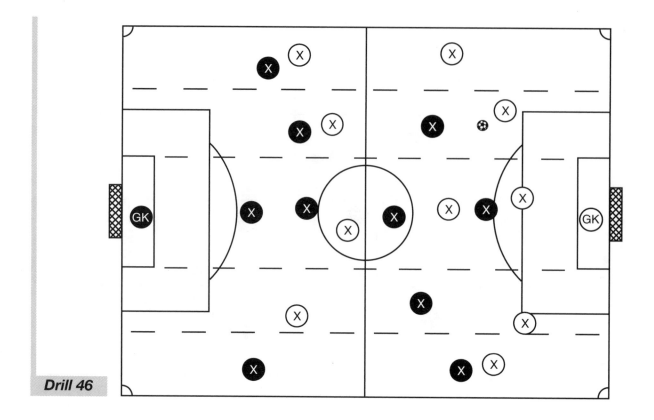

Drill 46

47 The Game

Purpose

To complete the practice session with an 8 vs. 8 or full match without conditions to assess what aspects of the session focus players have learned.

Organization

Set up an 8 vs. 8 or full match with all rules in effect.

Procedure

Organize two teams and play.

Key Point

Observe when the teams changed the point of attack and note when they should have changed the point of attack.

Variations

- Designate two or three players as playmakers with unlimited touches. Restrict the other players to one or two touches.

- Ask players to create an overload situation by making several passes within an area to draw defenders and then quickly switch play to the weak side for a penetrating attack on goal.

Drill 47

CHAPTER 6
Quick Counterattack and Transition Play

Dave Sarachan

D.C. United

We have all seen this before—a young player dribbles past an opponent, and just as he is about to shoot, he is dispossessed by an opposing player. Disappointed, the player who lost the chance to score drops his head and mentally drops out of the game. At the moment the play was over, could the player have helped his team by quickly recovering, becoming a defender, and winning the ball back? It happens at every level in every sport. When a team loses possession of the ball, everyone on the team must become a defending player. Simple, right? You'll agree that the concept of transition from attack to defense and defense to attack is paramount in the overall development of the soccer player.

What is transition and how is it important in soccer? Webster's dictionary defines transition as "a movement, development, or evolution from one form, stage, or style to another." An example of transition would be a team shifting from offense to defense or defense to offense. With youth players, the time gap between an attacking action and a defending action is huge. A young, developing player reacts more slowly from one movement to another than a player who has experience or is older. Players, as they develop and learn, reduce the gap considerably. How quickly youth players shorten this gap will depend on the soccer environment and training that they receive.

A great example of a successful youth training scheme is the Dutch system. At Ajax in Holland, youth players play small-sided (4 vs. 4) soccer in small areas of play. The action in these games encourages all players to attack while in possession of the ball and to defend when possession is lost. A game like this will expose a player who drops his or her head or is too slow to respond to a change of possession. There is no hiding in this exercise—all players are accountable for their actions. More important, playing against better players teaches something a coach cannot. Good teams and good players punish those who make a slow transition from attack to defense and defense to attack. Goals are scored. Is there a better way to convey a message or extend a reprimand than to have the opponent score against the player who is slow in transition? These moments generally come in quick transition and counterattack. Teams that quickly turn a defending action into an attacking action often create a numerical advantage for themselves. We all know that an ideal attacking action gives the team with the ball a numbers-up advantage, that is, 6 vs. 5, 5 vs. 4, 4 vs. 3, and so on.

Players and teams must have certain qualities to be effective in transition play and quick counterattack. First on my list is speed. The speed I mention is not just physical running speed—it is speed of thought and decision making. Players who possess running speed and technical speed have a great advantage in transition play, but a player who is quick in switching gears upstairs, who can read the next play early, who can execute technique on demand, will gain advantage with quick counters. Second, players must be technically proficient in three areas—short- and long-range passing, receiving, and running at speed while in possession of the soccer ball. We have all watched enough soccer games to recognize that successful counterattacking teams can play quickly in transition and can play balls over distance. The expression "It's not long ball if it lands to feet" is appropriate for teams that choose to play with counters in mind. Teams that look to counterattack must have certain characteristics within their 11 players. Counterattacking teams usually do well to keep their "shape" and have in their attack one, two, or three players with speed.

In training, coaches can provide an environment for players to develop speed of thought and quick play in transition from attack to defense and defense to attack. I have included training sessions that can help develop a player's ability to play and think quickly. I have always believed that the game is the best teacher and that it is our job as coaches to facilitate this philosophy. The games that I offer are useful and realistic to the bigger game of 11 vs. 11.

As I have moved from one level of soccer training (college) to another (professional), I have seen first hand how small the gap in transition can be. Teams that can switch gears quickly have a distinct advantage in punishing teams for their mistakes. In my practice sessions, you'll see a constant theme of small-sided training. Restrictions within these sessions can help improve areas that you, the coach, feel need improvement. One touch, two touch, switch of play . . . the list can go on. Here with D.C. United, in every training session we emphasize quick ball movement and honest soccer. Honest soccer? This is an expression for the actions of a player who knows that his or her role changes as possession changes. Keeping things simple and understanding the job of making the transition from attacker to defender—this is honest soccer (how often we have heard attacking players say, "It isn't my job to defend, I'm a forward!"). Developing these honest habits is our job as coaches. We must do more than just introduce these sessions. We must facilitate them—poking, tweaking, and prodding during training while developing an eye for seeing within the session proper form and execution.

48 9 vs. 9 With 20-Yard Offside Line

Purpose

To play over a bigger area with offside being only 20 yards from goal. This enables players in the attack to play deeper (even behind defenders).

Organization

Organize two teams of nine. The field is penalty area to penalty area. Form offside lines with disks 20 yards from the penalty box. Give players a side to defend and attack.

Procedure

1. Play the game to big goals, like a regular full-sided match.
2. Players can be in front of their line and *not* be offside (even if they are behind the last defender).
3. Play a regular game with free kicks, corner kicks, and so forth.

Key Points

- Look for teams to play quick balls forward and over the top of the defending team.
- See who takes advantage of the liberal offside rule with quick balls forward.
- Determine who can play quickly and play quality long balls.

Variation

Add a midfield line and restrict the team in their defending half to two touches. This puts the emphasis on defenders playing quickly and playing longer passes to teammates.

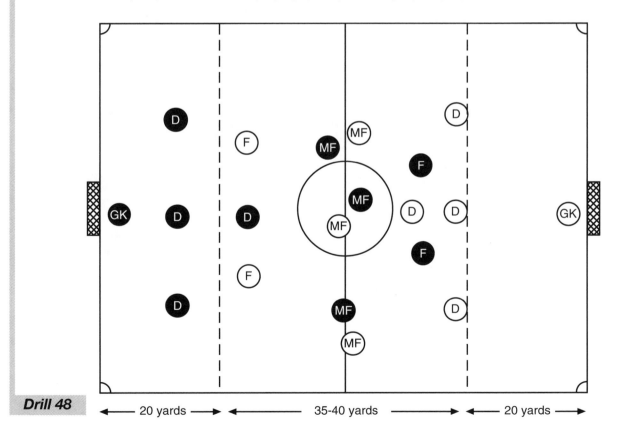

Drill 48 ←— 20 yards —→ ←——— 35-40 yards ———→ ←— 20 yards —→

49 Four-Goal Game With Small Goals and Two Neutrals

Purpose

To play to one of the two goal options and score.

Organization

The area of field is small, 45 by 35 yards, so that players learn to work in tighter space. Set up the goals with cones three to five yards apart. Use two teams of six; each team has two goals to attack.

Procedure

1. Set up the field in a 45-by-35-yard grid. Organize two teams to attack assigned goals.

2. Assign two players as neutral players who cannot score.

Key Points

• Look for teams and players thinking and reacting quickly to small advantage opportunities, for example, 3 vs. 2 or 2 vs. 1 to goal.

• Watch how quickly teams react to switch of play.

Variation

Add touch restrictions.

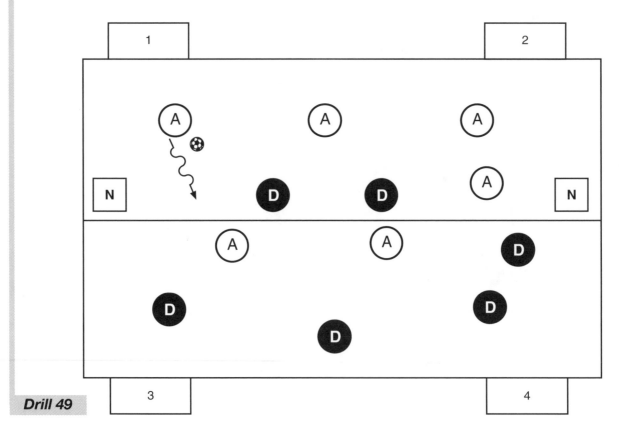

50 Four-Goal Game (Big Goals)

Purpose

To switch the point of attack and quickly counterattack to one or the other goal.

Organization

Arrange 8, 9, 10, or 11 vs. 11 from penalty area to penalty area. One team can attack either goal 1 or 2. The opposing team can attack either goal 3 or 4.

Procedure

1. Decide which team will attack which goals.

2. If your team has four goalkeepers, use one in each goal.

3. You can modify the activity if you have only two goalkeepers. One of the two goals would have a goalkeeper; the other would not. Players can score at the goal with no goalkeeper only by heading.

Key Points

- Look to see how teams react from offense to defense.
- Teams should look to switch play quickly when one goal shuts down.
- Look for quality finishing.

Variations

- Add a midfield line. A team will only get credit for their goal if the remaining teammates move to midfield. (This keeps teams compact.)
- Require a team to make 5 or 10 consecutive passes before allowing them to go to goal.

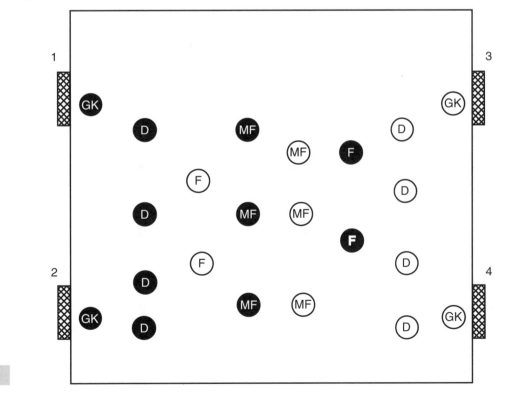

Drill 50

51 Small-Sided Game With End-Line and Sideline Neutrals

Purpose

To use width and depth with the extra players and to recognize quick advantages.

Organization

Divide players into three teams of six. Two teams take postions on a 60-by-50-yard field. From the third team, two players take positions on one end line, two take positions on the other end line, one goes to a sideline, and the last goes to the other sideline.

Procedure

1. The first team (X_1) starts and goes to the opposing goal. Either team can use any of the neutrals (X_3).

2. The sideline neutrals have a two-touch restriction, and the end-line neutrals have a one-touch restriction.

3. Switch teams when one team scores two goals.

4. The teams all rotate to be neutrals.

Key Points

- Encourage long passes behind defenses to end-line players. Defenders must turn and run with attackers.

- Look for teams to switch play and attack with speed.

- Look to score goals. How quickly do players use neutrals, and how fast do the players react?

Variations

- End-line and sideline neutrals *can* score. (They always must stay behind their respective lines.)

- Add touch restrictions to teams on the field.

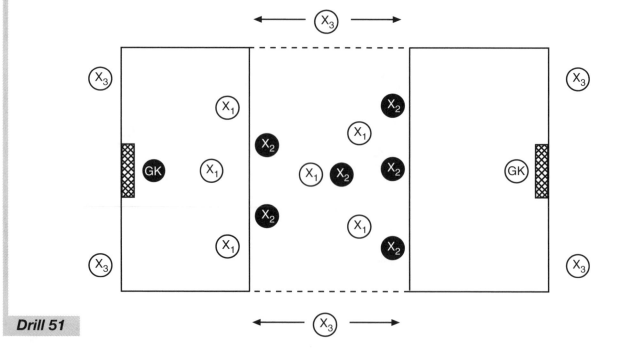

Drill 51

52 6 vs. 6 vs. 6 to Big Goals

Purpose

For one team to score. A team that wins possession from another team must successfully reach the neutral zone while in possession before it can attack the next team and goal.

Organization

Divide players into three teams of six, each in different colors. The field is 60 by 45 to 55 yards wide. A neutral zone, marked with disks, is 15 yards wide in the center of the field.

Procedure

1. Start with one team (X_1) attacking another (X_2).
2. If the X_2s steal, they must get past the X_1s and into the neutral zone while in possession of the ball.
3. The waiting team (X_3) stays on the other side of the neutral zone and awaits the next attacking team (in this case, the X_2s).
4. The X_2s try to beat the X_3s and score.
5. The game goes back and forth until a team reaches a predetermined number of goals.

Key Points

- Observe how quickly a defending team dispossesses and attacks into the neutral zone.
- Look for quick transition by players.
- Look for quality attacking actions and finishing.

Variations

- Add restrictions on touches.
- Include corner kicks (if the ball goes over the end line).

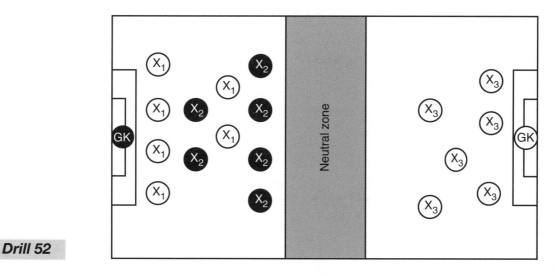

Drill 52

53 6 vs. 6 + 6 in Penalty Area

Purpose

To recognize same-color neutrals to help the team keep possession.

Organization

Divide the team into four groups of four, five, or six (shown as X_1, X_2, X_3, and X_4). (If it's 6 vs. 6 to start, one group wears vests of one color and the other wears vests of a different color.) The resting players spread out around the penalty area, with alternating colors next to one another.

Procedure

1. This is a possession game for the team in the penalty area that has the ball. Making 10 consecutive passes equals a goal.

2. A red-vested player, for example, can only use a red-vested neutral player for help in possession.

3. Switch teams after three or four minutes, depending on age.

Key Points

• Watch how quickly teams go from attack to defense.

• See who uses the neutrals effectively.

• Look for quality passing and movement, and quick interplay with each other on the field and the neutrals.

Variation

If you don't have enough players, use only one extra team of five or six as neutrals.

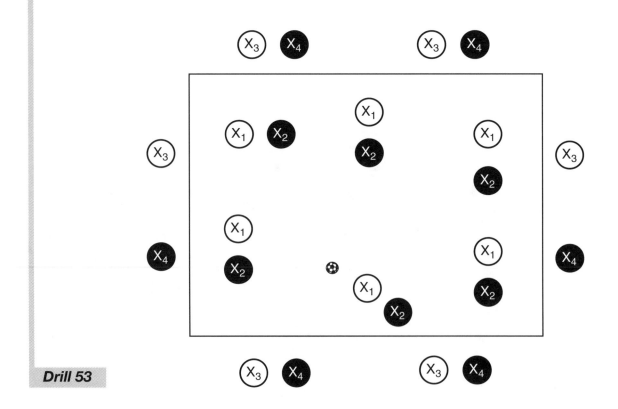

54 3 vs. 3 Transition Finishing

Purpose

For one team to score 10 goals first.

Organization

On a short field (25 yards long) one team of nine lines up on one end line. The opposing team of nine lines up on the other (not inside the goals). You will need two goalkeepers and many balls.

Procedure

1. Each team puts a team of three on the field. The coach starts by giving one team possession. Three play against three and try to score.

2. If the attacking team shoots and misses, the defending team returns to their end line. A new group of three players with a ball comes out and immediately attacks the first team. They try to score at the other end.

3. If a goalkeeper makes a save, he or she throws it back out to the three teammates already on the field. They keep playing until a shot misses or a goal is scored.

4. Whenever a shot is taken that goes past the goal or goes in, the defending team returns and a new group of three with a ball comes on and attacks.

Key Point

This is a fun, fast 3 vs. 3 transition game that involves quick thinking and quality finishing.

Variations

- Depending on the age group, you can shorten or lengthen the field slightly.
- Play to fewer goals than 10 goals depending on the age and skill of the group.

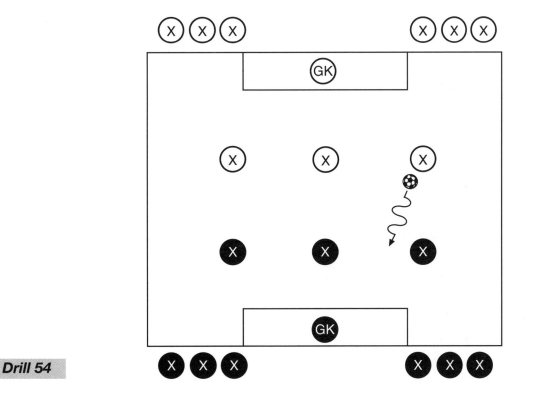

55 Multiple-Goal Game

Purpose

For teams and players to recognize an opening to goal and execute quality passing.

Organization

Set up eight goals by placing disks three yards apart on one-half of a field. The area of the grid should be 50 by 45 yards. Organize two teams and play 6, 7, or 8 vs. 8.

Procedure

1. One team spreads out and looks to go to any open goal.

2. Teams score by passing a ball from one side of the goal through the disks to a teammate on the other side.

3. Teams can score from either side, and two teammates can play back and forth until the opposing team interferes.

Key Points

- Look for heads up and switch of play.
- Players should spread out and pass quickly.
- Look for quality long-range passing.

Variation

You may need to add neutral players (who can't score) to help with possession.

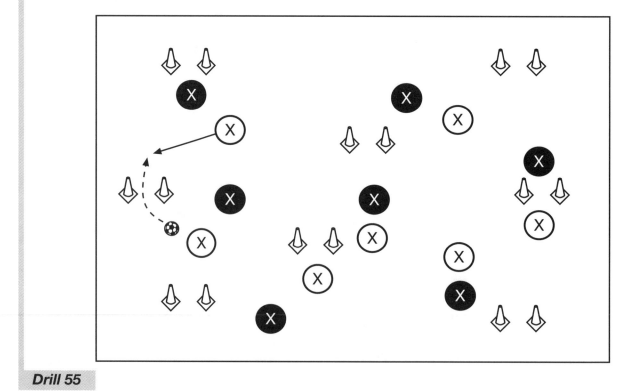

Drill 55

56   5 vs. 5 up to 7 vs. 7 With Extra Balls

Purpose

To keep possession as a team in a smaller area of the field and to be quick in reaction from offense to defense.

Organization

Organize a 5 vs. 5 in a 45-by-35-yard area. Use all extra balls, and spread them around the area evenly (the more balls, the better).

Procedure

1. Play a possession game of keep away.

2. When a team loses a ball, they must then defend.

3. When a ball goes outside the area, any player can use any of the balls around the area and immediately put it into play.

Key Points

- How well does the team in possession pass and connect?

- Which players and teams pause or stop when a ball turns over or goes out of bounds?

- Quick thinkers put a ball into play quickly and successfully connect passes.

Variations

- If you have a limited number of soccer balls, you can quickly throw one to the team that gets it next.

- Permit unlimited touches or play with two neutral players if the attacking team needs help.

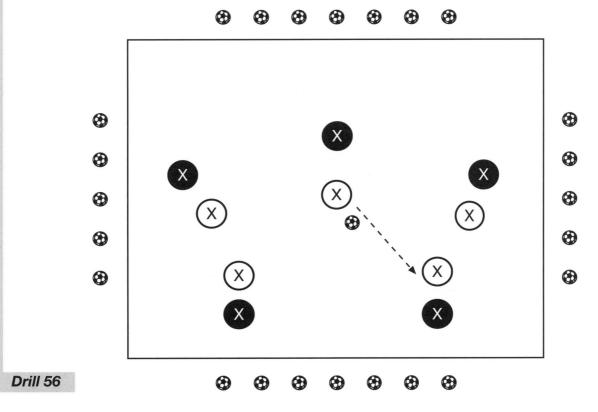

57 8 vs. 4 With Disks

Purpose

To keep possession with successful (5, 8, or 10 consecutive) passes against the four defending players.

Organization

Organize three teams of four, each team wearing different colored jerseys, for example, red, yellow, and blue (X_1, X_2, and X_3, respectively, in diagram). The teams play keep away inside the penalty area.

Procedure

1. Blue defends first. Each of the four blue-jerseyed players holds a training disk while they chase the other two teams that have joined forces to keep the ball from blue.

2. When any of the blue chasers steals, all four blue players drop their disks. Players on the team that just lost the ball (say yellow) must now run to pick up a disk before the other two teams keep possession for 10 consecutive passes.

3. Keep score by awarding a point to the team that connects with 10 consecutive passes.

Key Points

- Evaluate speed of reaction from defending to attacking.
- Evaluate how well teams connect passes with one another.
- Evaluate switch of play, passing, and moving.

Variations

- With younger or less technical players, permit unlimited touches.
- Adjust the number of passes that teams need—7, 8, 10, or even 15 for very good players.

Drill 57

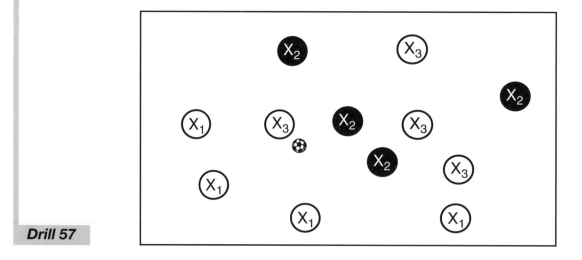

58 Three-Zone Practice Session

Purpose

To connect with players in all three thirds of the field.

Organization

Use two teams of eight—three in the defending zone, three in midfield, and two in the attacking zone. This drill is performed from penalty box to penalty box. Use goalkeepers in regulation goals.

Procedure

1. Start with the first team building together out of the back (or defensive zone). They must successfully complete a pass to zone 2 so that one of them can enter that zone, thus adding a player to the midfield.

2. The first team passes and moves until they make a successful pass to a teammate in the attacking zone.

3. A midfield player, after completing a successful pass to a teammate in the attacking zone, can enter to help attack and score.

Key Points

• Each player must pass and move through each zone. This exercise simulates realistic numbers in each zone at the start: +1 on defense, even numbers in midfield, and −1 in attack.

• Evaluate how quickly teams use their advantage in quick transition with extra players.

Variations

• Play two touch in the defensive zone and free (unlimited touches) in the midfield and attacking zones.

• Permit players to skip passes from defense into midfield and play longer balls up to their attackers. Any midfield player can then enter the attacking zone.

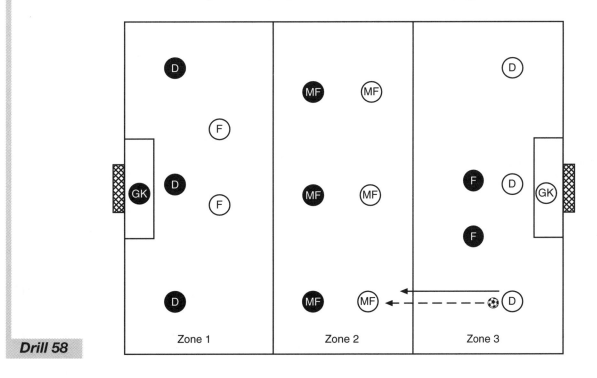

Zone 1   Zone 2   Zone 3

59   Team Counterattack 9 vs. 7

Purpose

To work specifically with an attacking team in practicing counterattacks to goal.

Organization

Play one team of nine (defending) vs. an attacking team (minimally seven, could be up to nine). The field can be regulation size. Use two big goals with goalkeepers.

Procedure

1. The defending team has a two-touch restriction, and the team with seven has unlimited touches.

2. At any point in the scrimmage, stop play.

3. Then allow the team with fewer players to play a free pass over the top of the defensive team. The defending team cannot touch the ball. When the attacking team receives the pass, the defending team can defend.

Key Points

- Watch for quality passes to attacking players

- Encourage quick movement of the ball

- Look for total attacking movement with all seven attackers. (In the diagram, one A can play a free pass over to another A. This will allow counterattack options.)

Variations

- Look for counterattack options from both teams.

- The defenders must move to midfield to get credit for a goal. Allow the goalkeeper for the attacking team a free distribution pass, either kicking or throwing.

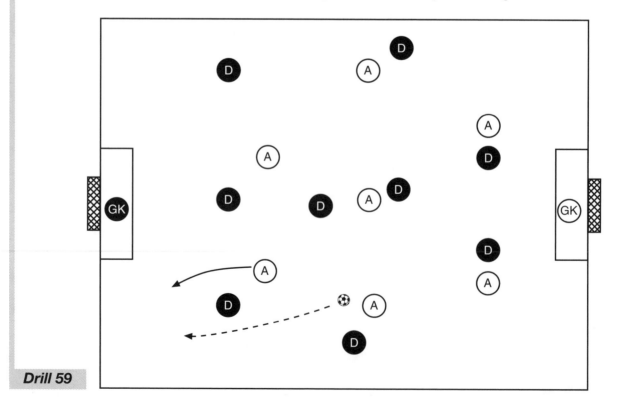

Drill 59

CHAPTER

7

Attacking on the Flanks

Jay Hoffman

U.S. Soccer Federation

Flank play has always been a significant aspect of the game. Over the past several years it has become even more important as opponents commit more players to defending, defend with lower restraining lines, and organize players centrally in their system of play with greater defensive responsibilities. Attacking and exploiting the space on the flanks by individuals and groups of players can provide a team with opportunities to pull apart the opposition's defense and create goal-scoring chances.

As the game has evolved, responsibilities and functions of individuals and groups of players have increased, changing the attacking and defending posture of teams. These new systems of play enable players to exploit the space on the flanks more effectively.

In the beginning most of the wide play was left to the winger, who had attacking responsibilities only. Today this can still happen, depending on the ability of a player or players and how the team is organized around these players. It has become more difficult, however, to exploit this space consistently with only one player. Coaches have organized, experimented, and trained various playing combinations to exploit the opposition on the flank—wingers, unorthodox wingers (players who function as wingers but play deeper in the scheme of the team), flank midfielders, flank defenders, and marking backs who can push into the attack. We have seen various creations and modification of systems of play. We have also seen a focus on zonal defending, allowing these players to position themselves earlier to take advantage of space on the flank.

In developing the team and to enhance possibilities of attacking on the flank, coaches must first select players who individually can exploit this space and the opponent. Realizing that each player has different competency in the physical, psychological, technical, and tactical components of the game, coaches must evaluate these qualities to determine the players best suited for playing in flank positions.

Although competition, coaching, and training can improve a player's ability, coaches would like to select players who have the physical and psychological dimensions that permit them to be successful in attacking on the flank. Physical dimensions for flank players include running speed, agility, acceleration, quickness, power, vertical jump, and both aerobic and anaerobic endurance. Psychological aspects include confidence in one's technical ability, an inclination to take risks, the ability to overcome failure, a goal-scoring mentality, unselfishness on both sides of the ball, and mental toughness.

The components of technique and tactics depend strongly on each other. Although all players must be technically competent under pressure, flank players have specific technical demands. These technical requirements include the ability to beat opponents by dribbling; to turn balls both on the ground and from the air; to cross and execute bent- and flat-ball services to near-post, central-post, and far-post areas; to hold the ball under pressure; and to pass accurately in combination play, both in and out of the box, and over long distances to change the point of attack. The ability to finish with all surfaces and both feet, to head the ball for goal scoring, and to lay balls off for others are the technical functions of flank players. Players should work to improve these technical skills with the nondominant foot to add to their effectiveness in beating the opposition on the flank, to both the outside and the inside.

Players can improve these specific technical skills through technical functional training in each third of the field under pressure of an opponent.

As players become more technically competent under pressure, their tactical ability, range of play, and speed of decision making provide them with the opportunity to alter the game. In attacking on the flank, a player's tactical functions are first determined by the demands of the game in the specific thirds of the field and are associated with the safety risk factors of play. The system of play and the number of players in flank positions, such as a winger, deep-lying winger, wide midfielder, outside back, or marking back, will also affect tactical situations. Although the game will demand specific tactical functions of the flank players by their position, every wide player confronts these situations. To be effective, flank players need to be trained and knowledgeable in all facets of play.

A wide player, whether playing as an outside back, outside midfielder, or winger, performs numerous tactical functions. Although some of these functions vary according to the thirds of the field and where players are positioned, the principles remain the same. Players must be able to execute them as they play themselves through the thirds of the field.

Common tactical functions include establishing and maintaining width in attack through the thirds of the field; beating opponents off the dribble and through combination play; choosing, placing, and timing services into the box from the flank; creating space both with and without the ball for themselves (to face the goal) and for others; providing support behind, laterally, and in advance of the ball; maintaining team shape in relation to the position of the ball while attacking; and exploiting the opponent immediately after winning the ball, either by playing the ball forward or by taking the space by dribbling.

A specific tactical function for the outside back in attacking the flank space would be to establish a good defensive starting position. This increases the back's ability to intercept the ball, take advantage of the opposition's attacking shape, and make the transition to counterattack. The number and position of other players playing on the flank will influence tactical decisions.

The flank midfielder's tactical functions can be influenced by the positioning of players on that side of the field and whether a player is behind the flank midfielder as a defender, in advance as a winger, or both. The functions of the flank midfielder greatly expand in a 3-5-2 system, where the back may not be able to attack because of defensive responsibilities.

Playing as a winger or withdrawn winger and the organization of the team behind this player can affect the player's tactical functions. You can expand the flank player's tactical options by placing the player on his or her nondominant side of the field, so the player's strength is to come to the inside, creating space for others and giving them greater opportunities to score goals. These players will also need to be competent playing with their backs to the goal and in central positions.

Technical and tactical functional training, based on these functions, provides players with the opportunity to read and solve situations on the flank so that they can exploit the space and the opposition. The following are some examples of functional training that will help the team become proficient in attacking on the flank.

Perform the following exercises on the appropriate side of the field with players in their playing positions. The exercises must replicate the game demands of the positions being trained. Develop the activities to game speed. Add pressure incrementally to make the activities like the game.

60 Functional Fitness Crossing and Defensive Recovery

Purpose

To develop physical and psychological competence.

Organization

This activity requires flank players, a goalkeeper, two or three attacking players, and a server. You will need 10 to 15 balls, a goal, and cones.

Procedure

1. The flank player starts 40 yards from the goal. The server plays the ball down the line into the space for the flank player to run on to and cross, finding one of the attackers in the box to finish.

2. The flank player immediately sprints back to the line.

3. The server plays the next ball, and the flank player repeats the exercise, doing as many repetitions as possible in a given unit of time.

Key Point

Alter the work-rest ratio of the exercise bouts depending on the level of fitness and the system to be trained.

Variations

- Increase the distance from the goal for the sprint, depending on the player being trained—winger, midfielder, or flank defender.

- Have the server change the angle of serve.

continued

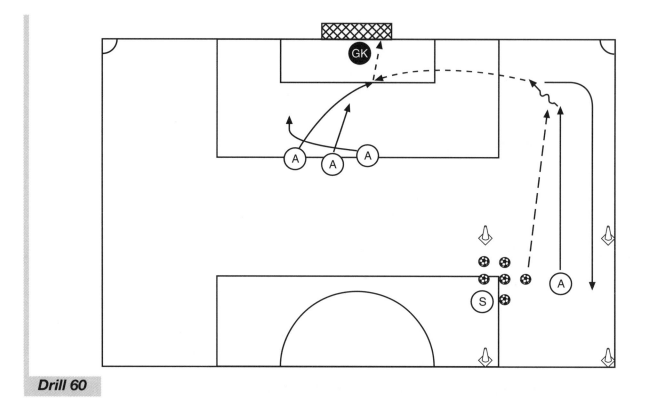

Drill 60

61 Functional Fitness Crossing and Defensive Recovery to 1 vs. 1

Purpose

To develop physical and psychological competence.

Organization

This activity requires flank players, a goalkeeper, two or three attacking players, two or three attacking players on the flank, and a server. You will need 10 to 15 balls, cones, bibs, and a goal.

Procedure

1. The flank player starts 40 yards from the goal. The server plays the ball down the line for the flank player to run on to and serve to attacking players in the box.

2. Upon completion of the service, an attacking player starts dribbling from the end line to the halfway line, trying to score by getting between the cones on the halfway line.

3. The flank player who served the ball must recover and prevent the attacking player from getting to the line (1 vs. 1).

4. If the flank player wins the ball he or she then sprints down the line and serves again. The next attacker (dribbler) starts from the end line.

continued

5. If the flank player does not win the ball, if it goes out of bounds, or if the attacker scores, the server serves another ball for the flank player to cross, and the recovery run begins again.

Key Point

Alter the work-rest ratio of the exercise bouts depending on the level of fitness of the players and the system to be trained.

Variations

- Vary the position of the server playing balls down the line.
- Vary the recovery distance for the 1 vs. 1 flank play, making it specific to the position—winger, midfielder, or defender.
- Change the time of starting the attacking player down the line to play 1 vs. 1.

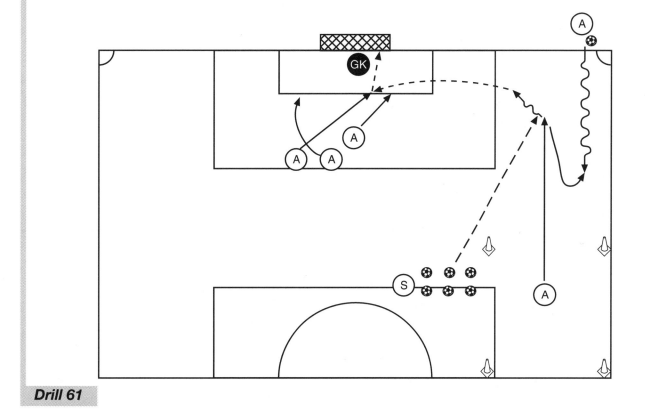

Drill 61

62 Functional Fitness 1 vs. 1

Purpose

To develop physical, psychological, and technical competence of both the flank attacker and the defender.

Organization

This activity requires flank players, a goalkeeper, two or three attackers, and defenders. You will need 10 to 15 balls, bibs, and a goal.

Procedure

1. The flank player positions between the 18-yard box extended and the sideline. The server plays the ball to flank player's feet, who turns and faces the defender.

2. The defender works to prevent the flank player from beating him or her or serving the ball.

3. When the ball is served or played out of bounds, the next ball is served to play 1 vs. 1 again.

Key Point

Alter the work-rest ratio for the exercise bouts depending on the level of fitness and the system to be trained.

Variations

- Flank player plays 1 vs. 2.

- Increase the distance from the goal to play 1 vs. 1. Begin 18 to 30 yards from the goal with the same width of the field.

- Allow defenders to deny flank players the ball or prevent them from turning.

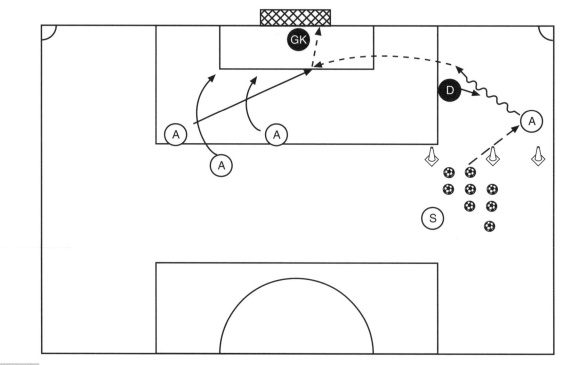

63 Technical Functional Training Finishing

Purpose

To develop technical competence in finishing and receiving from the flank position.

Organization

This activity requires flank players, one or two goalkeepers, defenders, and servers. You will need 15 to 20 balls, bibs, one or two goals, and cones.

Procedure

1. Play in the attacking third of the field (30 to 40 yards). Use both ends of the field for more repetitions.

2. The server plays the ball to the flank player, who is checking for the ball in a wide position with body open to the field. The flank player receives the ball across the body to face the goal.

3. The flank player dribbles at a cone or player, plays to the inside or outside, and finishes. As the player becomes more proficient, have a defender shadow the attacker and then play 1 vs. 1 to the goal.

Key Points

- Observe how players receive—their choice of surface and the quality of the first touch.
- Observe how players finish—their selection of technique to finish, body position, balance, and weight transfer.
- Notice when players choose to finish under pressure.

Variations

- Alter the angle and distance for the flank player to receive and attack the goal.
- Have balls served to the flank player at various angles, heights, and distances.
- Add a second defender to play 1 vs. 2 to the goal.

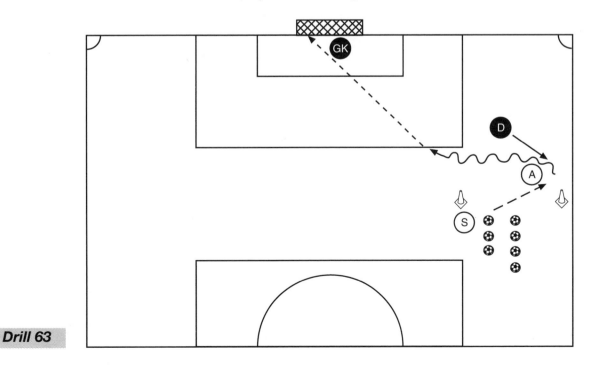

Drill 63

64 Crossing Off of Speed Dribbling

Purpose

To develop competence in technical aspects of crossing when dribbling for speed and in the execution of various types of crosses.

Organization

This activity requires flank players, one or two goalkeepers, two or three attacking players in the box, defenders added to the attacking players in the box (one to three), defenders to pressure the crosser, and servers. You will need 15 to 20 balls, bibs, cones, and one or two goals.

Procedure

1. Play in the attacking half of the field. The length of the sprint with the ball can vary.

2. The server plays the ball in front of the flank player, who runs onto it and dribbles with speed, crossing it when appropriate for a chance on goal.

Key Points

- Observe technical aspects of dribbling for speed, body position, contact of the ball by either the shoelaces or the outside of the foot in a running position of the foot.

- Look for correct preparation of the ball for crossing and the final touch for crossing.

- Observe technical aspects, body position, and foot placement in the type of ball crossed—bending, driven, on the ground, chipped, cut back, or far-post cross.

- Note tactical implications.

Variations

- Progressively add defenders to the attackers in the box, creating 3 vs. 1, 3 vs. 2, and 3 vs. 3.

- Add a chaser to the flank player.

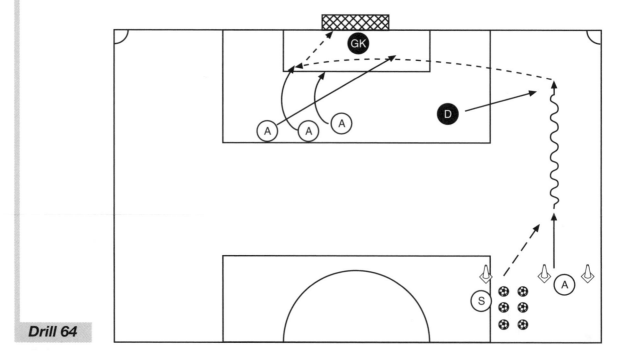

Drill 64

65 One-Touch Crossing

Purpose

To develop technical aspects of crossing without preparation of the ball and technical aspects in the execution of various types of crosses.

Organization

This activity requires flank players, one or two goalkeepers, two or three attacking players in the box, defenders (one to three) added to the attacking players in the box, defenders to pressure the crosser, and servers. You will need 15 to 20 balls, bibs, cones, and one or two goals.

Procedure

Play in the attacking third or attacking half of the field. Servers play balls down the line for the flank player to run onto and cross with one touch.

Key Points

- Note body position to cross the ball and technical aspects in the execution of various types of crosses driven, chipped, far post, bending, on the ground, and cut back.
- Observe body mechanics, balance, and foot placement.
- Note tactical implications.

Variations

- Vary the angle of ball service.
- Vary the distance the ball is served down the line.
- Progressively add defenders to the players in the box, creating 3 vs. 1, 3 vs. 2, and 3 vs. 3.
- Add a chaser to the flank player so he or she is under pressure to cross.

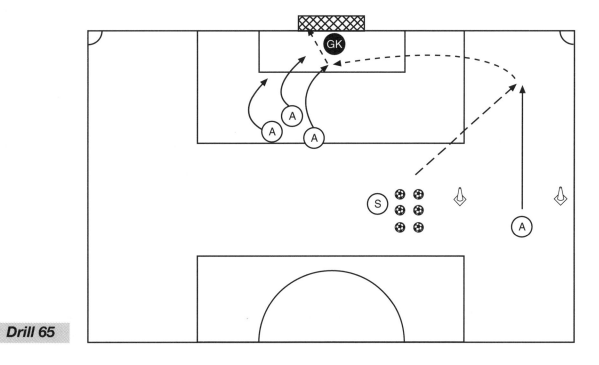

Drill 65

66 Technical and Tactical Functional Training 1 vs. 1

Purpose

To develop technical and tactical competence on the flank to either cross, finish, or get behind the opponent.

Organization

This activity requires flank players, wingers, midfielders, defenders, two or three attacking players in the box, defenders vs. attackers in the box, defenders on the flank, one or two goalkeepers, and servers. You will need 15 to 20 balls, bibs, and one or two goals.

Procedure

1. The flank player under pressure of an opponent (use shadow defense to begin) creates space to turn the ball and face the defender. The server plays the ball in.

2. The flank player takes on the opponent and beats the defender to either the outside or inside to cross, finish, or play.

3. Develop the defender to play full pressure as in the game. Have flank players do repetitions.

Key Points

- Observe technical aspects of receiving, dribbling, crossing, passing, and finishing.
- Note tactical implications of technique.
- Observe tactical aspects of creating space, beating an opponent, and play in the attacking third.

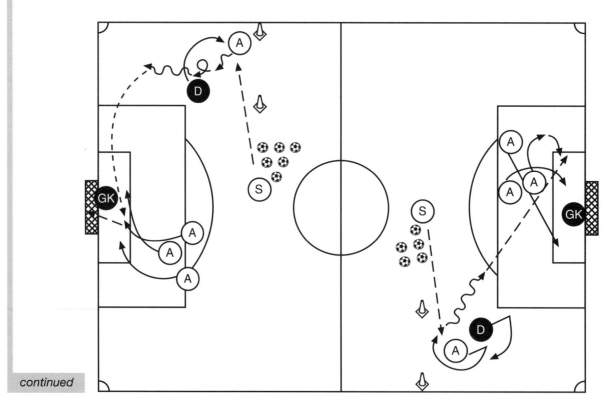

continued

Variations

- Add defenders to the attacking players in the box to create 3 vs. 1, 3 vs. 2, 3 vs. 3, and 3 vs. 4.
- Add a second defender to defend the flank player.
- Vary the angle and type of ball served to the flank player.
- Play continuously from end to end. When the defense wins the ball, they play to their flank player at the opposite end.

Drill 66

67 Combination Play—Wall Pass With Variations

Purpose

To develop play among players in the attacking third of the field, combining to get the flank player behind the defense. To develop technical and tactical aspects of combination play.

Organization

You can do this activity with as few as five players or with the entire team playing both ways. You will need 15 to 20 balls, bibs, one or two goals, and cones.

Procedure

Activity A

This activity focuses on wall passing with the player in advance of the ball. The flank player creates space by checking off the defender so that he or she can receive the ball and be facing the defender. Once in this position the flank player runs at and takes on the defender. At the same time a forward shows in advance of the ball for a wall pass. The forward can show to the inside so the flank player can use the space wide, or the forward can show wide to allow the flank player to use the space inside. The flank player plays the ball to the forward and then runs behind the defender to receive the ball from the forward (one-touch pass) for either a cross, pull back, or shot. Begin this activity with the defender or defenders playing in shadow status until the flank player has grasped the concepts.

Activity B

This activity focuses on wall passing with a player who supports laterally or behind the flank player. The flank player receives a ball where he or she is not able to create space to turn on the defender. Play the ball to this player even though the player is marked. The flank player shields the ball from the defender while dribbling away from the direction in which he or she wants to go, creating space behind the defense. The support player, either lateral or behind, finds an angle where he or she can receive the ball and at the same time be able to play the ball behind the defense. The flank player plays to the support player creating the wall; spins and goes behind the defense; and receives the ball with one touch from the wall, allowing the flank player to attack the goal, cross, pull back, or finish. Begin this activity with the defender or defenders playing in shadow status until the flank player has grasped the concepts.

Key Points

- Look for technical aspects of receiving, dribbling, crossing, finishing, and passing.
- Observe tactical aspects of playing 2 vs. 1, timing of runs, angles and distance of support, implication of technique, creating space, principles of attack, transition, and vision.

continued

Variations

- Add defenders to players in the box.
- Add players in the midfield to both the attacking and defending teams.
- Play continuously going both ways.

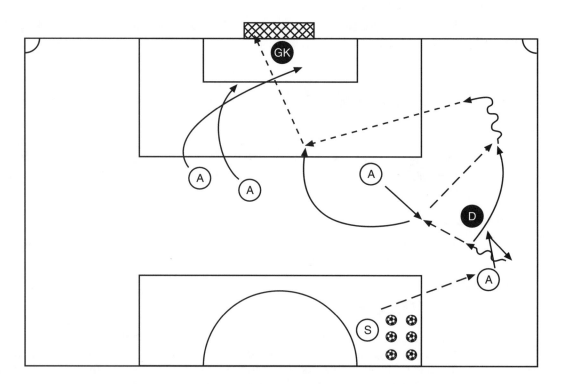

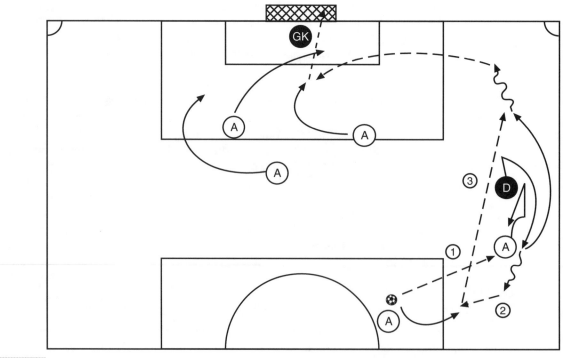

Drill 67

68 Double Pass

Purpose

To develop interplay that will get the flank player behind the defender. To develop technical and tactical aspects of combination play

Organization

You can do this activity with as few as five players or as many as the entire team playing both ways. You will need 15 to 20 balls, bibs, cones, and one or two goals.

Procedure

1. The flank player combines with a central midfielder, or possibly a central or wide defender, for a double pass to get behind the defender.

2. The ball begins with the support player, who plays the ball to the flank player, who is checking but under pressure from the opponent. Play the ball to this player, who lays it off first time to the support player.

3. The support player has taken up a supporting angle and distance so that he or she can play the ball behind the defender of the flank player, first time and into space for the flank player to run on to.

4. After playing the ball to the support player, the flank player spins away from the direction he or she played the ball and gets behind the defender to receive the ball and go to goal, cross, pull back, or finish.

Key Points

- Observe technical aspects of receiving, passing, finishing, dribbling, and crossing.

- Note tactical aspects of playing 2 vs. 1 double pass, timing of runs, angles and distance of support, vision, transition, attacking principles of play, implication of technique, and creating space.

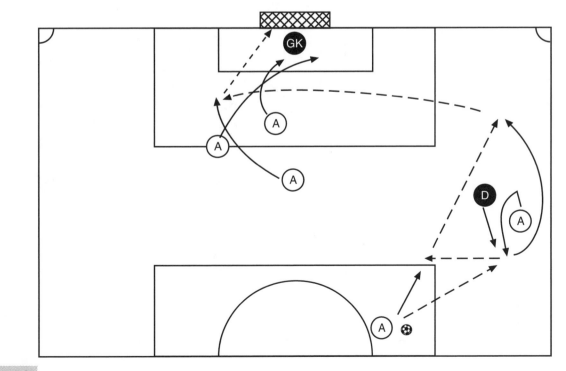

continued

Variations

- Add defenders to the players in the box.
- Add players to both teams and play both ways to make it more gamelike.

Drill 68

69 Technical and Tactical Functional Training—Overlap

Purpose

To develop the ability of flank players to create space for another player to use in getting behind the defense on the flank.

Organization

You can do this activity with as few as five players and as many as the entire team playing both ways. You will need 15 to 20 balls, bibs, cones, and one or two goals

Procedure

1. The flank player creates space on the flank for another player to use in getting behind the defense.

2. A support player—wide defender, flank midfielder, or central midfielder—plays the ball to a flank player in advance of the ball, who has checked and created space to turn and face the defense.

3. Because he or she wants to create space on the flank, the flank player, now with the ball, runs at the defender, taking the defender central to goal, thus creating space on the flank for the support player.

4. The support player runs behind the player with the ball, who times a pass into space for the support player to get behind the defense without allowing the defense to

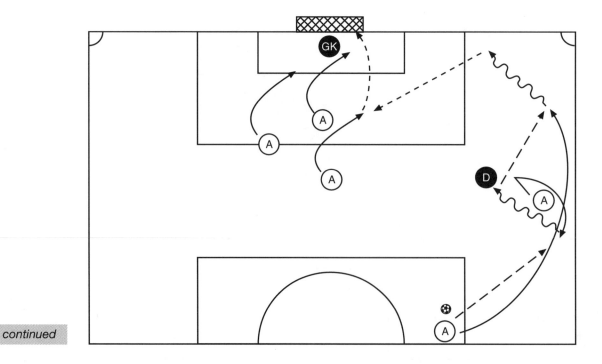

continued

react. This permits the support player to attack the goal, finish, cross, or pull back for attackers in the box.

5. To begin this activity, have the defender play in shadow status to allow the flank players to grasp the concepts.

Key Points

- Observe technical aspects of passing, crossing, finishing, dribbling, and receiving.

- Note tactical aspects of creating space, implications of technique, supporting angles and distance, timing of runs, transition, vision, and attacking principles of play.

Variations

- Add defenders to the attacking players in the box.

- Add players to both teams to play both ways.

Drill 69

70 Game for Flank Play

Purpose

To develop technical and tactical competence of the flank players on both sides of the ball, with the emphasis on attacking.

Organization

Use team organization with 16 field players and two goalkeepers. You can modify the activity and use fewer players as long as you train the flank players. You will need 10 to 15 balls, bibs, cones, and two goals.

Procedure

1. Play on a field that is 75 yards wide by 70 to 80 yards long. Each team plays 4 vs. 3 in their attacking half of the field. The attacking players play only in this half.

2. The defensive team is allowed to push a wide defender into the attacking half to attack on the flank in an overlap.

3. The two central midfielders play both ends, producing a 5 vs. 4 in each team's attacking half of the field, plus the potential of the defender coming forward.

4. Players should be looking for flank play to create goal-scoring opportunities in this game.

Key Point

Observe technical, tactical, physical, and psychological aspects of the game for the flank players on both sides of the ball.

Variations

- Play with the 18-yard box as the offside line.

- Let the flank players for both teams play both ends of the field all the time.

- Allow more players to go forward, meeting the demands of the game.

- Play the offside rule as stipulated.

- Organize the players according to the system your team plays.

continued

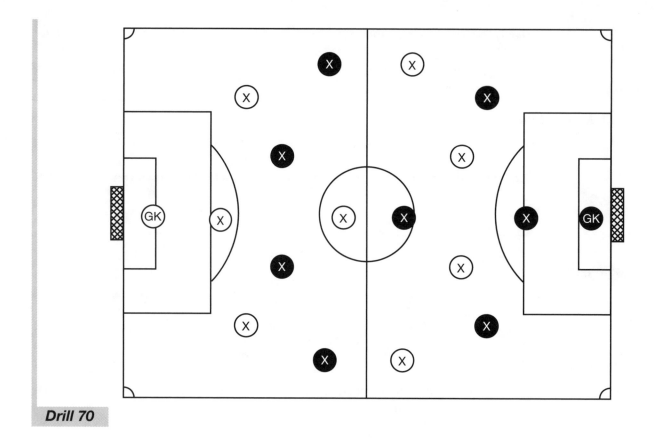

Drill 70

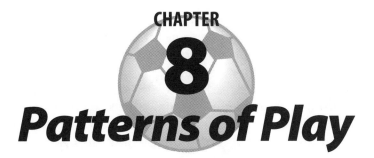

8
Patterns of Play

Stephen Locker

Harvard University

The intrigue of soccer is one of the game's greatest attributes. We love being entertained by creative players, seeing things we didn't expect to see. Our challenge as coaches is to facilitate this imagination and, at the same time, provide enough order to ensure that we score more goals than our opponents.

We usually start by establishing a system (or formation) based on the characteristics of our players. The coaching schools all tell us that this is how it should be done. I operate contrary to this thinking. As a collegiate coach, I have found that I rarely have the same 11 players available for every game. My experience tells me this is true at most levels. If we design a system around 11 players and then change one or more them, our system becomes obsolete. With this in mind, I have adopted a system that I believe is sensible and, more important, one that I feel competent in coaching.

Once we choose our system, we ask all our players to learn and understand the demands of every position. This allows us greater flexibility in replacing players. Note that although we ask players to understand all the roles and functions of every position, we still match players with positions that embody their particular characteristics. One of the skills of the coach remains his or her ability to recognize a player's characteristics and to put that player in the correct position. We are now ready to establish *patterns of play.*

Patterns of play are simply our plan for moving the ball toward our opponent's goal. Activities that teach patterns of play have the potential to be less stimulating than some of the small-sided games, shooting exercises, or possession games that make up the greater portion of our training regimen. This does not have to be the case. I have incorporated into my repertoire of training exercises a series of activities that I believe are stimulating, functional, and effective in establishing patterns of play. The degree to which you allow player creativity and expression to remain within your system is based on your style of teaching.

We begin our season by establishing a solid understanding of our system during preseason. One of the things we like to do is walk through several situations by taking the team onto the field after dinner. We remain in our street clothes and limit our activity to walking. We create an environment of open discussion and encourage players to ask questions about their particular movements. The players have come to enjoy this opportunity to gain a better understanding of their roles.

Once the season begins, we periodically reinforce our patterns. Pregame training sessions are also an important time to work on patterns of play. These exercises offer us an opportunity to solidify our tactical plan while saving valuable energy for the upcoming game.

What follows is a series of exercises designed to teach patterns of play. My philosophy in teaching patterns is to keep it simple. Complicated tactics only make your opponent's job that much easier. It is the speed and timing of play that make it difficult for an opponent to stop you.

(71) Six-Goal Soccer

Organization

Between the 18-yard line and the midfield line, place three goals on each touch line. Goals are one yard wide.

Procedure

1. First, play 10 minutes walking only.

2. Then play 10 minutes running. Limit all players to one touch. Play 10 vs. 10.

Key Points

- Arrange players in your formation.

- During the walking phase of this exercise, you do a lot of teaching about how you want your team to move the ball. Because the players are limited to walking, they are able to see the field of play better and thereby make better decisions.

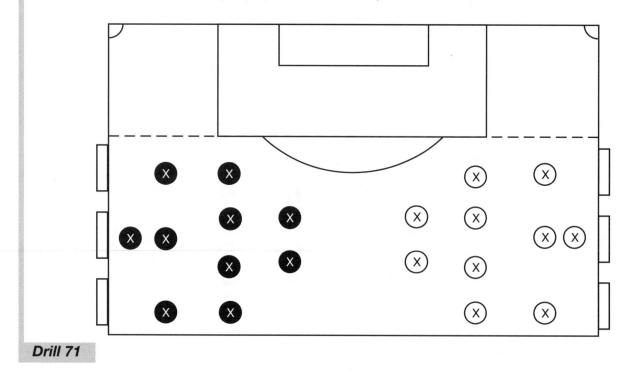

Drill 71

72 Shadow Drill to Goal

Organization

Set up the field as shown, with flags representing player positions as the team goes from the middle third to the attacking third. A goalkeeper is in goal, but no defenders are used. Set up coaches (or servers) as shown. Players start next to flags based on their positions; extra players are also next to flags ready to go on the next turn.

Procedure

1. The coach behind the midfield line starts play by sending a pass out to the outside defender.

2. The passes follow as diagrammed. Two additional passing sequences follow on succeeding diagrams. Use each passing sequence for 10 to 15 minutes.

3. Once the original ball has been shot on goal, the coach next to the goal serves a ball and calls out the name of the player whom he or she wants to shoot. The coach does this twice, to simulate a rebound opportunity.

4. Immediately, the coach on the side plays a ball to the withdrawn defender, who plays one touch to a target player at the top of the box.

5. The target player plays a wall pass, and the defender shoots first touch. A total of four shots are taken.

Key Point

Besides teaching patterns of play, this exercise is excellent for stressing one-touch passing and getting many runners into the box.

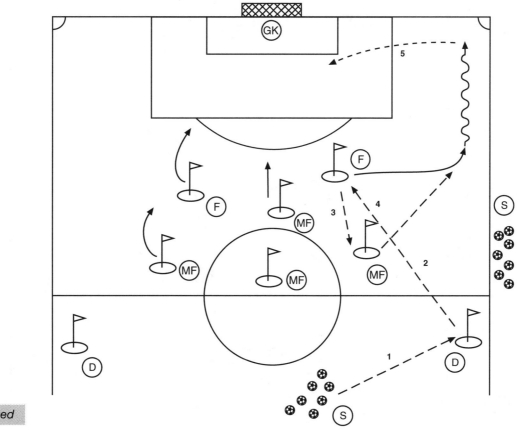

continued

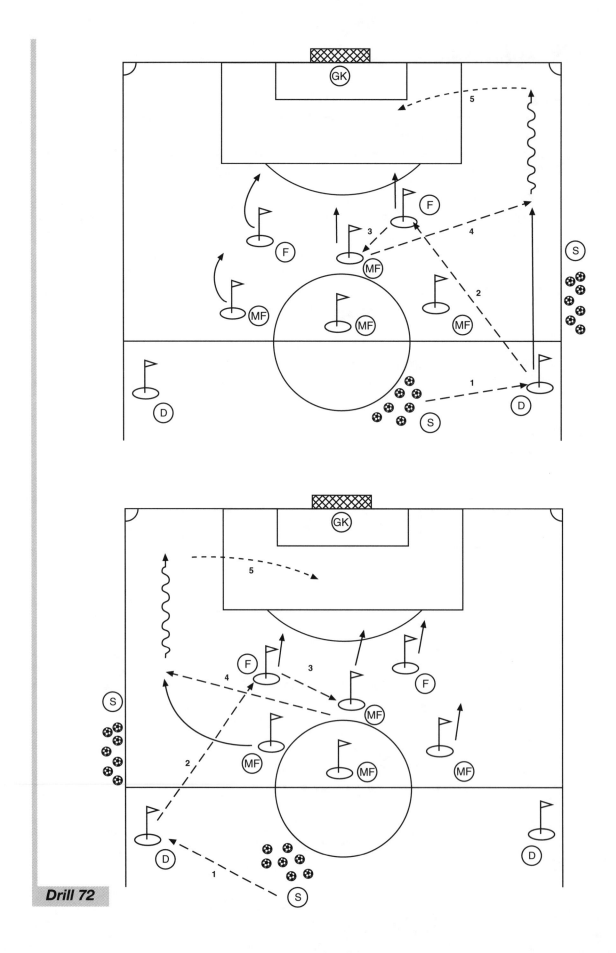

Drill 72

73 Patterned Runs to Create Penetration

Procedure

1. Two coaches, indicated by C, position themselves as shown. A player with the ball begins by dribbling at the coach and then passing back to the center midfielder.

2. Players follow the passing sequence as diagrammed.

Key Point

It is important that attacking players, the opposite midfielder, and at least one central midfielder get into the box as targets.

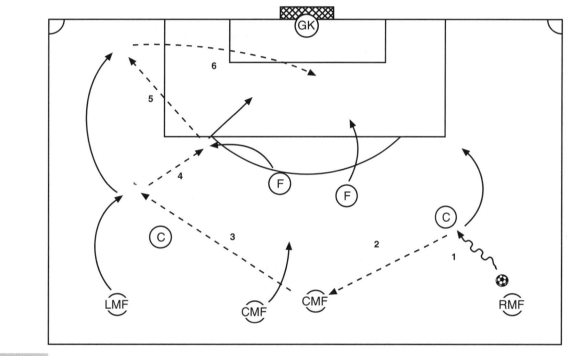

Drill 73

74 Patterns for Width in Attack

This drill follows the pattern in drill 73 except that you add additional flank players. Follow the pattern of play as diagrammed. This drill is effective in promoting forward movement by outside defenders.

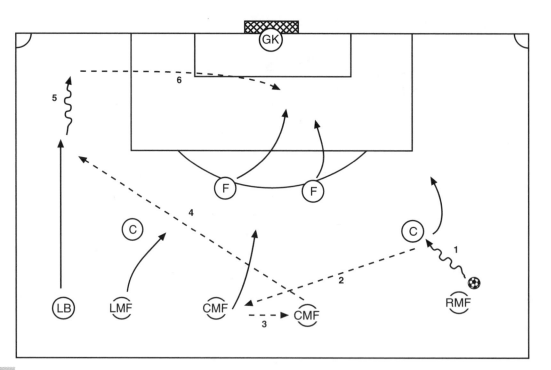

Drill 74

75 11 vs. 1 on Half Field

Procedure

1. Players operate without opposition (except for the opposing goalkeeper).

2. Game speed is required, although for initial use I recommend walking through patterns of play.

3. The ball can start with the goalkeeper, and building out of the back is developed. The coach has the option to direct this exercise in ways that best serve the team.

Key Point

Use a half-field to allow more sequences and do less running. The result is more learning in less time.

continued

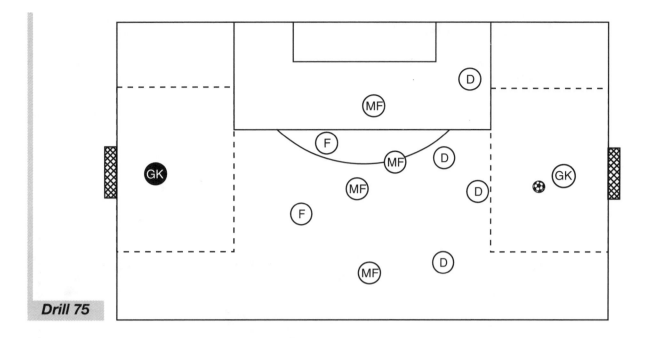

Drill 75

76 11 vs. 11, 50-by-50-Yard Grid, Team Handball

Procedure

Rules for this drill are

1. no running with the ball,

2. the ball must be passed within one or two seconds,

3. no contact,

4. players can only intercept passes,

5. any ball dropped goes to the opposing team, and

6. players must score with a volley off a pass.

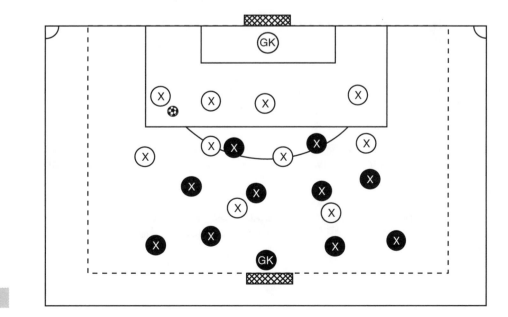

Drill 76

77   11 vs. 11 on Half Field

Coaches stand on opposite touch lines to call offsides. Play one touch for 10 minutes and then open it to unlimited touch for 10 minutes. Always emphasize speed of play.

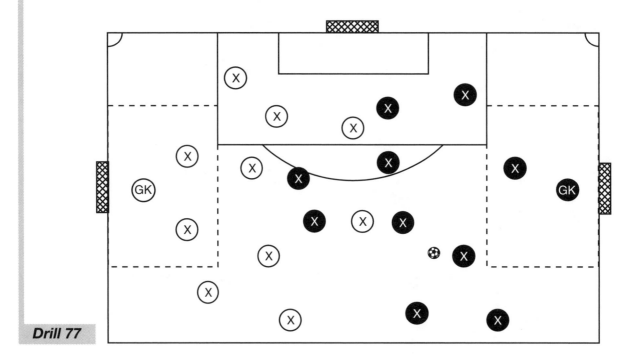

Drill 77

78   Possession Soccer With Five Goals

Organization

The field is 18-yard line to 18-yard line and 44 yards wide. The goal in midfield has three sides.

Procedure

1. All players participate, up to 11 vs. 11.

2. Points are scored by successfully passing the ball through either side of any goal to a teammate.

3. Play three 15-minute games with a pause between each game. Game 1 is three touch, game 2 is two touch, and game 3 permits unlimited touches.

Key Point

Pattern-of-play development takes place because of goal placement. This diagram depicts the area of the field where we like to move the ball.

continued

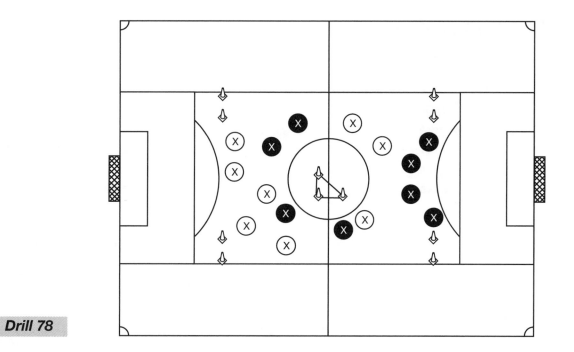

Drill 78

79 5 vs. 5 With Supporting Players in Flank

Procedure

1. Play directionally toward the 18-yard line and the midfield line.

2. Players can pass to flank players only after three consecutive passes in the middle.

3. Score one point for crossing the opponent's line under control.

Key Point

This exercise stresses short, quick combination passes in the middle, followed by a long ball to the flank, which then opens up the play.

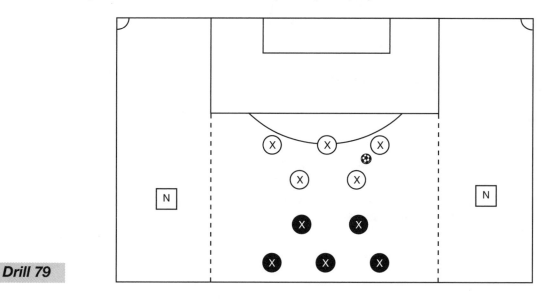

Drill 79

80 Creating Penetration Via Target Players

Procedure

1. Four players line up across the field. The advanced central player is designated the target (T) player.

2. The withdrawn central player plays a long ball to the wide player.

3. The wide player plays the ball to the target player, who plays it back to the central midfielder.

4. The players repeat the sequence to the other side as they continue down the field. The target player moves constantly from side to side to provide close support.

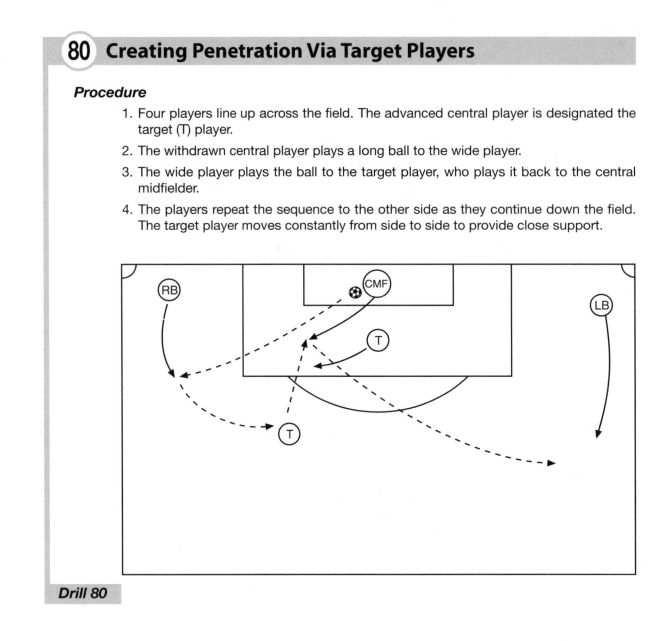

Drill 80

81 Attacking Combinations

Procedure

1. This time we have two central players playing side by side.

2. X_A plays long to X_B, and X_B plays short to the trailing X_C player. X_C then plays long to X_D, and X_D plays short to the trailing X_A player.

3. The players repeat this down the field and finish with a combination pass in the corner and across. Use near-post and far-post runs, with a trailer at the top of the box.

continued

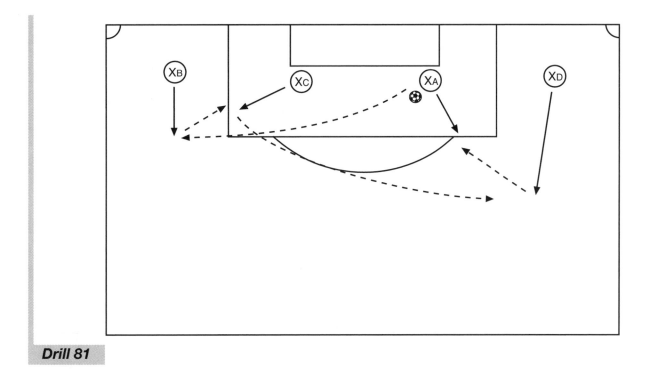

Drill 81

82 Penetration of the Attacking Third

The diagrams show two passing combinations used from the middle third going into the attacking third. You can easily devise additional patterns of play to fit your desires.

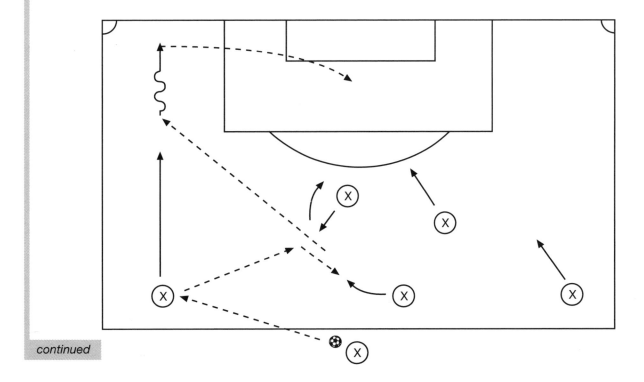

continued

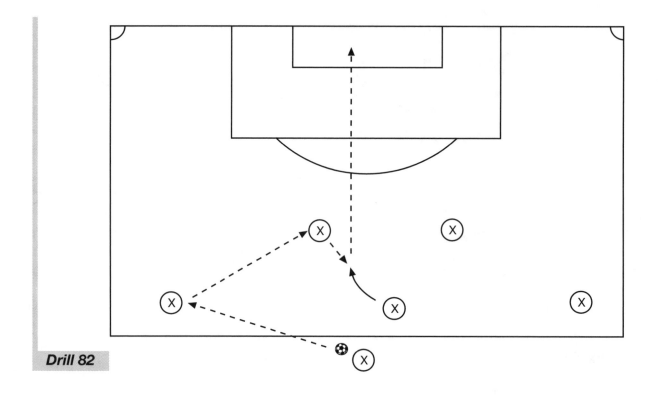

Drill 82

PART
III

Attacking From Restart Plays

Restarts encompass a variety of dead-ball situations that include but are not limited to free kicks, corner kicks, and throw-ins. A large percentage of goals scored at higher levels of play originate off restart situations, so it follows that training should be devoted to organizing and perfecting the team's ability to score from set pieces.

In chapter 9 Gene Klein, head soccer coach at Quaker Valley High School and assistant coach for the professional Pittsburgh Riverhounds (A League), provides an in-depth analysis of corner kick and throw-in plays. Successful execution of a corner kick requires an accurate serve, proper timing and placement of player runs, and individual determination and commitment to get on the end of a crossed ball. Although teams may choose from a variety of corner kick plays, they are usually grouped into three general categories. The far-post corner is designed to exploit the space near the goal post most distant from the ball. The ball is flighted toward the far side of the goal, generally 8 to 12 yards out from the end line. Patterned player runs before and during the serve are designed to clear space and free an attacker for a strike on goal. The near-post corner attacks the space on the side of the goal nearest the ball. The ball is generally driven low and hard toward the corner of the six-yard box. Players time their runs to intercept the flight of the ball and deflect it on goal. A third option is the short corner. Rather than serving the ball into the goal mouth, the kicker passes the ball to a teammate nearby, who has the option of dribbling toward the goal or serving a ball into the goal area. Teams usually use the short corner as a change of pace from the normal corner kick routine.

Coach Klein also discusses using the throw-in as a scoring weapon. Although the primary function of a throw-in is to return the ball into the field of play after it has traveled out of bounds over a touch line, in some instances a team can use it to create scoring opportunities. Most teams have one or more players who can toss the ball a great distance, sometimes all the way from the touch line into the center of the goal area. Long throws are difficult to defend and create an attacking situation similar to a corner kick.

In chapter 10 Sam Koch of the University of Massachusetts discusses the planning and execution of free-kick plays. Indirect and direct free kicks provide the opportunity to execute a planned play, or, in its simplest form, the chance to strike a stationary ball at goal. Coach Koch provides a number of possible free-kick options. Coaches are urged to use their creativity and ingenuity to devise their own variations. Regardless of individual differences, all free-kick plays should conform to the following guidelines:

- **Simplicity**. Keep the play simple. The more complex and intricate the plan, the less likely it is to work! As a rule, use one or two passes to create a strike at goal.

- **Organization**. Each player must understand his or her role in the free kick.

- **Deception**. Movement before the kick, including dummy runs over the ball, may cause defenders to readjust their positions and create open space in which to strike the ball on goal.

- **Test the goalkeeper**. A free kick that does not produce a shot at goal is a failure.

CHAPTER 9
Corner Kicks and Throw-Ins

Gene Klein
Quaker Valley High School

Statistics indicate that restarts, or dead-ball situations, provide some of the best opportunities in soccer to create goal-scoring chances. Depending on the level of play, some studies show that 30 to 40 percent of all goals are scored from a restart, with a significant portion of those from throw-ins or corner kicks.

The reasons for this are really twofold: first, many players have the athleticism and skill to throw the ball great distances and serve corner kicks with accuracy and velocity; second, corners and throw-ins are special situations in soccer in which a coach can repeatedly rehearse specific plays. Functional practices can ultimately enhance individual and team proficiency in these areas. Because corners and throw-ins initiate dangerous goal-scoring opportunities, it is important for you to develop training activities that replicate game situations. Specific practices for corner kicks and throw-ins are important not only for technical and tactical concerns but also for spectator appeal. The excitement of the crowd builds every time a team is about to take a corner kick. If a team has a player with a strong, accurate throw into the penalty box, everyone from spectator to opponent is focused on that moment. Players need to realize that games can be won or lost in these situations.

You need to consider taking and possessing throw-ins from the defending third, the middle third, and the attacking third of the field. Several points are important in each area. Maintaining team shape is crucial to any throw-in taken from the defensive third. Should your team be dispossessed after a throw-in, they must immediately be able to defend with numbers. Another consideration is the choice between playing safe, short, simple passes to maintain possession or making long throws to get the ball upfield into the opponent's territory with a higher risk of losing possession.

In the middle third of the field you should train your team to respond quickly to the ball out of bounds and execute a quick throw or exploit a defensive weakness with a long throw into the attacking third of the field. Often the long throw at midfield can take advantage of a defensive lapse because either the opponent's defenders are disorganized or space is available behind them to create an effective attack on goal.

It is in the attacking third where the best chances emerge. For throw-ins, essentially you can consider two strategies—a quick throw or a long throw. The element of surprise is a key. An alert player and team can execute a quick throw that can take advantage of a team still in transition from offense to defense or disorganized over their marking responsibilities. A quick, short throw that emphasizes possession may result in an early cross or perhaps an effective combination play that can lead to an early strike on goal. A quick throw to a talented 1 vs. 1 player can allow him or her to improvise and penetrate a defense with the dribble, which is usually a dangerous and exciting attacking play.

The effectiveness of the long throw in the attacking third depends on several factors, the most important being whether you have a player who can throw the ball for distance, accuracy, and velocity. Other considerations may apply. If your team does not have players who can consistently win the throw-in or a second or third ball in the air, it is probably better to maintain possession. If the opponent has a dominant goalkeeper or several prevailing defenders, a long throw might be futile because loss of possession would be likely. Long throw-ins are not as frequent at higher levels because those teams usually have goalkeepers and defenders who can consistently win those balls. Weather might also be a consideration. If you believe that the long throw can be an effective attacking weapon, there is no substitute for well-timed, well-choreographed runs. Players should throw balls to specific target areas, with precisely timed runs. Players should also be in position to attack the second and third balls that come off a defender from a head or clearance.

Corner kicks are similar to long throw-ins because much depends on the quality of the service and the abilities of the defending team. Consider inswinging or outswinging balls as well as short or long corners. Deploy players in the areas where the defending team is vulnerable or where your attacking players are strong. Still, you must consider team shape and balance. Discussion can center on serving balls to specific areas and timing runs into those spaces. In general, attackers should make runs to the near post, far post, and the central part of the goal. The location of the service, the velocity and swerve on the ball, and the timing of runs into those areas are crucial to any success for attacking corners.

Because corners and throw-ins create scoring chances, there is no question that it is helpful to rehearse runs and serves into specific areas. Quality of service remains an obvious key. If your team does not have a player who can consistently serve accurate balls into the danger areas, then you should emphasize possession passes. If you have a player who can serve wickedly accurate corners or throws and have the supporting players to attack balls in the air, then you should rehearse the more direct plays. Whether playing short or long, the team must maintain shape and balance to prevent counterattacks. At the same time you should be aware that too much regimentation can make attacks predictable and defensible. Therefore, when organizing practice situations for corners and throws, you should strike a balance between organization and creativity, for that is the key to all soccer tactics.

When practicing the throw-in drills, keep in mind the following key points.

- Organize players where they will be the most dangerous, regardless of position. (Positions are used in the diagrams for organizational purposes only.)

- Flank players should generally take throws because they are most likely to be closest to the ball. Quick throws, however, are beneficial; do not suspend play just to get a flank player in position.
- Whenever possible use players with ability to throw long.
- Runs from key players should be similar most of the time, so the entire team knows everyone's role.
- Emphasize that although just one to three players might be directly involved, everyone needs to be alert and moving off the ball so that all options are available for an effective attack.
- Encourage improvisation.

For the corner kick drills, consider these key points:

- Organize players where they will be the most dangerous, regardless of position.
- Runs should be to the key areas—near post, far post, and central part of the goal—although the key players should alter their runs and adjust angles to avoid being too predictable.
- Players should take positions to cover each third of the penalty area—the first third (end line to the goal area), the second third (the goal area to the penalty spot, or 12-yard spot), and the final third (the 12-yard spot to the edge of the penalty area).
- Emphasize that although just three or four players might be making runs to the goal, everyone needs to be alert for the second and third balls that have deflected off an attacking player or that a defending player has not fully cleared.
- Emphasize constant adjustment of runs to react to the serve and the positioning of the defenders. Runs need not be from long distances. Sometimes short, precise, explosive movements are better.
- Encourage improvisation.

When practicing the throw-in drills, follow this pattern of player and pressure variations:

1. 11 vs. 0—unpressured throw-ins with timing of runs and execution of various options
2. 11 vs. 3—three defenders added around the ball to force players to use certain options
3. 11 vs. 6—pressure added in the specific area of the throw-in to force the team to play out of that pressure using different options
4. 11 vs. 11—using passive pressure
5. 11 vs. 11—using full pressure in a controlled scrimmage

For the corner kick drills, use this pattern:

1. 11 vs. 0—unpressured corner kicks with timing of runs and execution of various options
2. 11 vs. 3—three defenders added to cover the near post, far post, and central part of the goal
3. 11 vs. 6—pressure added in the penalty area, forcing the team to adjust their runs and serves

4. 11 vs. 11—using passive pressure but forcing the team to adjust their runs and serves

5. 11 vs. 11—using full pressure in a controlled scrimmage

(83) Short Throw-Ins From the Attacking Third

Purpose

To practice timing of runs to the ball and off the ball for quick, effective, attacking throw-ins from the attacking third of the field, which will create a quick strike on goal.

Organization

Full-field practice, using a 4-4-2 system

Procedure

1. Set balls down just outside both touch lines. Direct a throw-in from a specific location, forcing the team to make some quick decisions and some quick adjustments in positioning.

2. Rehearse option 1. Throw to the first forward. The central midfielder stays behind the ball to support the thrower. The opposite central midfielder bends away to the goal. One forward breaks to the thrower, and one prepares a diagonal run behind the checking forward to the near post. The thrower should throw to the first forward, who plays back to the thrower or the central midfielder or, if open, turns and dribbles to the end line. Regardless of the decision, the second pass should immediately be served into the box to players running off the ball.

3. Rehearse option 2. Throw to the central midfielder. The central midfielder stays behind the ball and receives the ball from the thrower. The opposite central midfielder bends away to the goal. One forward breaks to the thrower, and one checks to the central midfielder receiving the ball. The central midfielder should play quickly to the thrower, the first forward, or the second forward. Regardless of the decision, the second pass should immediately be served into the box to players running off the ball.

4. Rehearse option 3. Throw to the outside defender. The central midfielder stays behind the ball to support the thrower. The opposite central midfielder bends away to the goal. One center back goes into space vacated by the second central midfielder. One forward breaks to the thrower, and one checks to the central midfielder closest to the ball. The thrower should play the ball back to the outside back, attempting to draw the defenders out of the defensive third and causing them to lose their shape and compactness. The outside back should play quickly to the thrower, the first forward, the second forward, one of the midfielders, or the center back. Regardless of the decision, the second pass should immediately be served into the box to players running off the ball, either by a cross or a through ball.

continued

Option 1

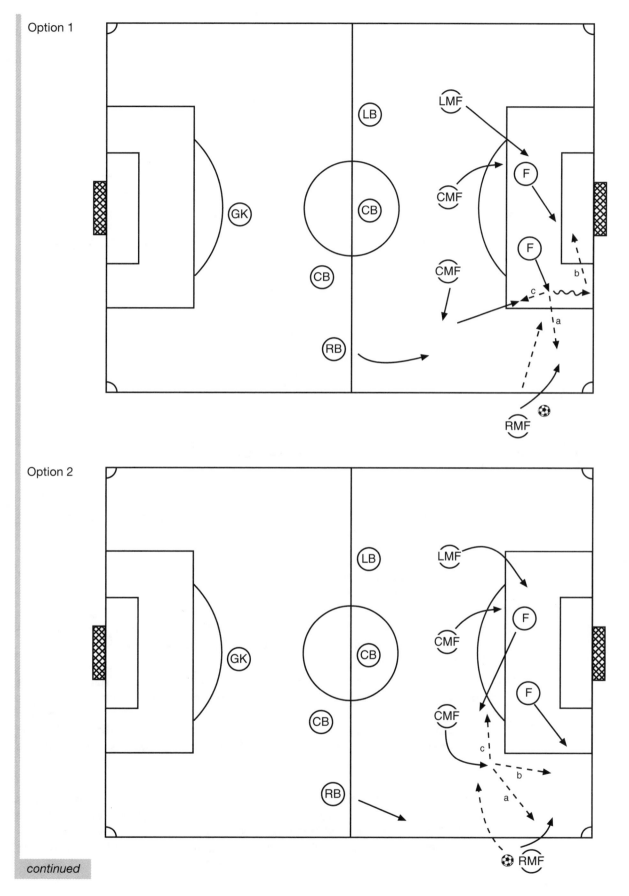

Option 2

continued

Option 3

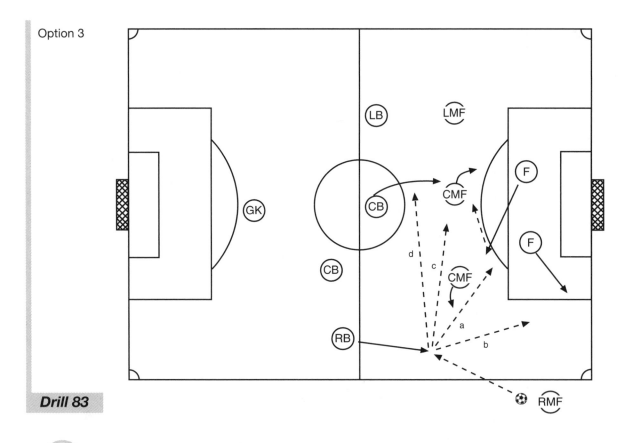

Drill 83

84 Long Throw-Ins From the Attacking Third

Purpose

To practice timing of runs to the ball and off the ball for long, effective, attacking throw-ins from the attacking third of the field, which will create a quick strike on goal.

Organization

Full-field practice, using a 4-4-2 system

Procedure

1. Set balls down just outside both touch lines. Direct a throw-in from a specific location, forcing the team to make some quick decisions and some quick adjustments in positioning.

2. Rehearse option 1. Throw to the first forward for a "flick." The central midfielder stays behind the ball to support the thrower. The opposite central midfielder bends away to the goal. One forward breaks to the thrower, and one prepares a diagonal run behind the checking forward to the center of the goal. The thrower should throw to the first forward, who flicks the ball back to the second forward or the central midfielder for a shot on goal.

3. Rehearse option 2. Throw to the center of the goal. The central midfielder stays behind the ball to support the thrower. The opposite central midfielder streaks to the goal. One forward breaks to the thrower and then bends away to the far post. The forward farthest from the ball runs across the goal, hoping to clear space for other players. Other players run to the goal. The thrower should throw directly to the first open player. All players should be alert for a second ball played by the receiving player.

continued

Option 1

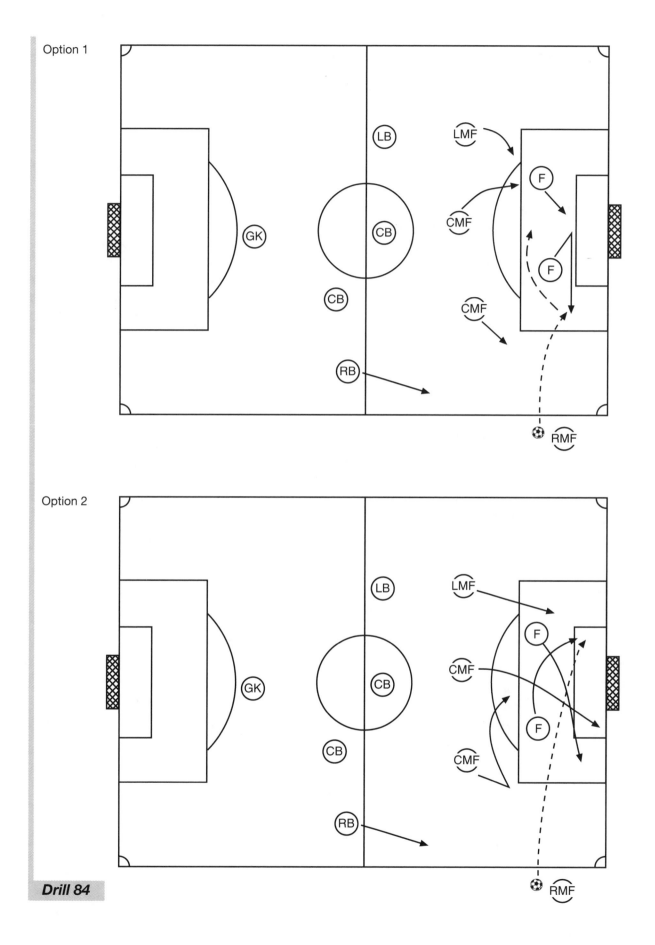

Option 2

Drill 84

85 Short Throw-Ins From the Midfield Third

Purpose

To practice timing of runs to the ball and off the ball for effective, attacking short throw-ins from the midfield third of the field, which will allow ball possession.

Organization

Full-field practice, using a 4-4-2 system

Procedure

1. Set balls down just outside both touch lines. Direct a throw-in from a specific location, forcing the team to make some quick decisions and some quick adjustments in positioning.

2. Rehearse option 1. Throw to the forward. The outside midfielder checks to the thrower along the touch line and then breaks down the flank. The center back stays behind the ball to support the thrower. The central midfielder also checks to the thrower. One forward breaks to the thrower, and one prepares a diagonal run behind the checking forward. The thrower should throw to the checking forward. The receiving forward should play early to one of the supporting players, preferably one of the midfielders, who then plays early to the second forward or the flank midfielder breaking to the goal on the counterattack. The central midfielder can also switch the point of attack to the opposite flank midfielder.

3. Rehearse option 2. Throw to the central midfielder. The outside midfielder checks to the thrower along the touch line and then breaks down the flank. The center back stays behind the ball to support the thrower. The central midfielder also checks to the thrower. One forward breaks to the thrower, and one prepares a diagonal run behind the checking forward. The thrower should throw to the central midfielder, who should play early to one of the supporting players, who then plays early to the corner and the

Option 1

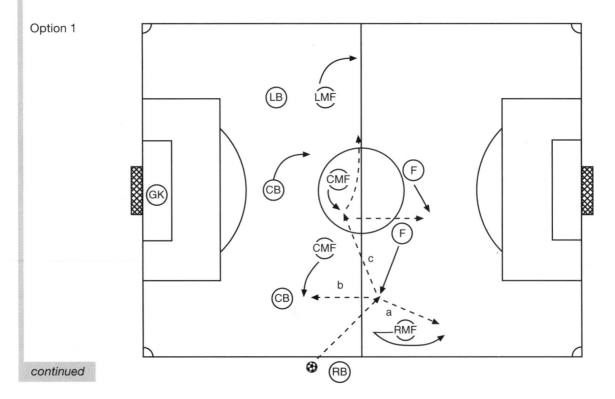

continued

flank midfielder breaking to the goal on the counterattack or switches the point of attack.

4. Rehearse option 3. Throw to the center back. The thrower should throw to the center back, who should play early to one of the supporting players or switch the point of attack.

Option 2

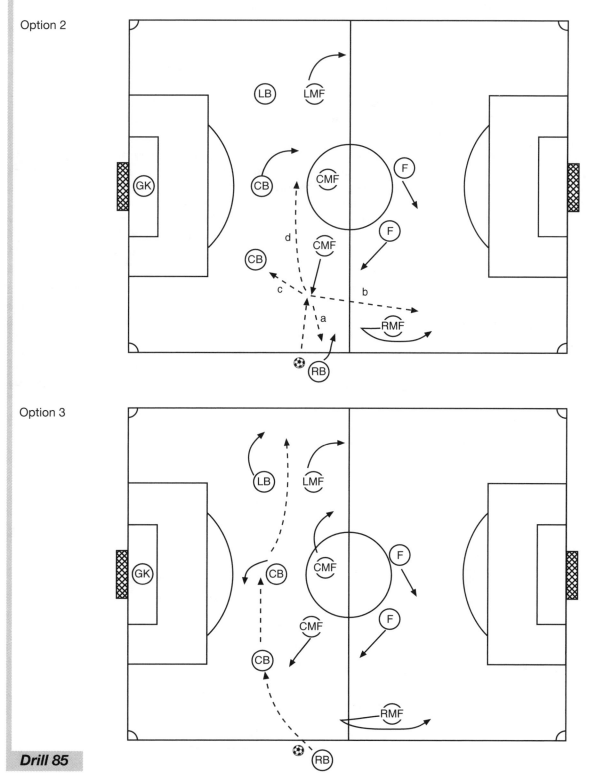

Option 3

86 Long Throw-Ins From the Midfield Third

Purpose

To practice timing of runs to the ball and off the ball for effective, attacking long throw-ins from the midfield third of the field, which will allow for a quick counterattack.

Organization

Full-field practice, using a 4-4-2 system

Procedure

1. Set balls down just outside both touch lines. Direct a throw-in from a specific location, forcing the team to make some quick decisions and some quick adjustments in positioning.

2. Rehearse option 1. Throw to the flank midfielder. The outside midfielder checks to the thrower along the touch line and then breaks down the flank. The center back stays behind the ball to support the thrower. The central midfielder also checks to the thrower. One forward breaks to the thrower, and one prepares a diagonal run behind the checking forward. The thrower should throw to the outside midfielder after he or she has faked checking to the thrower and should then break down the flank. The receiving midfielder should play an early cross to one of the other streaking players for a quick counterattack.

3. Rehearse option 2. Throw to the second forward. The outside midfielder checks to the thrower along the touch line and then breaks down the flank. The center back stays behind the ball to support the thrower. The central midfielder also checks to the thrower. One forward breaks to the thrower, and one prepares a diagonal run behind the checking forward. The thrower should throw over the head of the checking forward to the second forward on a diagonal run behind the first forward. The receiving forward should go directly to the goal or play an early cross to one of the other streaking players for a quick counterattack.

Option 1

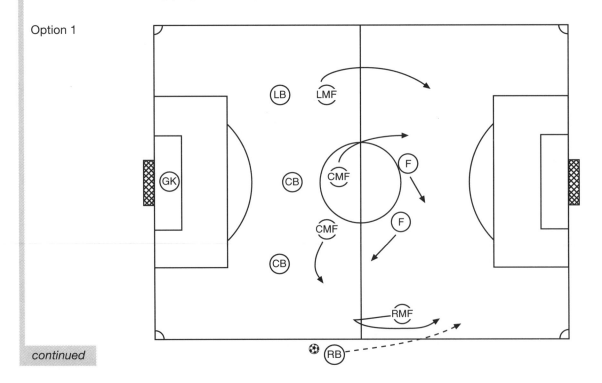

continued

Option 2

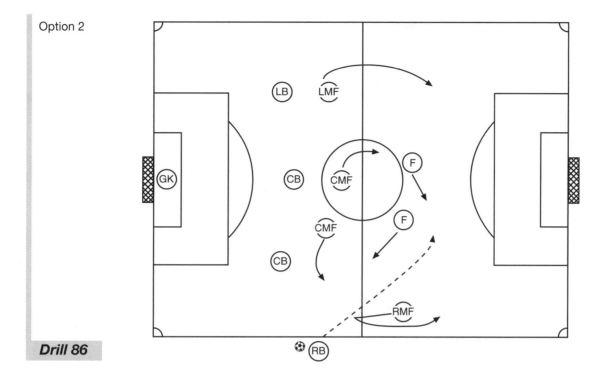

Drill 86

87 Short Throw-Ins From the Defensive Third

Purpose

To practice timing of runs to the ball and off the ball for effective, attacking throw-ins from the defensive third of the field with the intent of maintaining ball possession.

Organization

Full-field practice, using a 4-4-2 system

Procedure

1. Set balls down just outside both touch lines. Direct a throw-in from a specific location, forcing the team to make some quick decisions and some quick adjustments in positioning.

2. Rehearse option 1. Throw to the flank midfielder. The outside midfielder checks to the thrower along the touch line and receives the throw. The center back stays behind the ball to support the thrower. The central midfielder also checks to the thrower, looking for a ball back from the outside midfielder. One forward breaks to the corner flag, and one checks to the flank midfielder receiving the throw, so he or she can be played an early ball. If the central midfielder or the forward receives the ball, he or she should play early to the other forward or the other central midfielder to relieve the pressure.

3. Rehearse option 2. Throw to the central midfielder. The outside midfielder checks to the thrower along the touch line. The center back stays behind the ball to support the thrower. The central midfielder also checks and receives the throw from the outside back. One forward breaks to the corner flag, and one checks to the central midfielder receiving the throw so he or she can be played an early ball. The central midfielder receiving the ball should play early to one forward or the other central midfielder to

continued

relieve the pressure by switching the point of attack. Any ball played back to the center back should be immediately played out, perhaps to the outside midfielder or by switching the point of attack.

4. Rehearse option 3. Throw to the center back. The sequence is the same as in options 1 and 2, but the ball is played back to the center back, who then immediately plays it out, perhaps to the outside midfielder, a forward, or one of the central midfielders, who would switch the point of attack.

Option 1

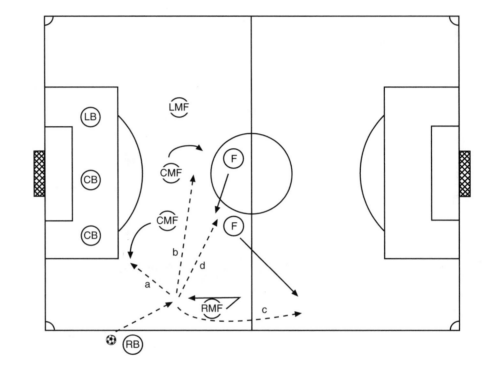

Option 2

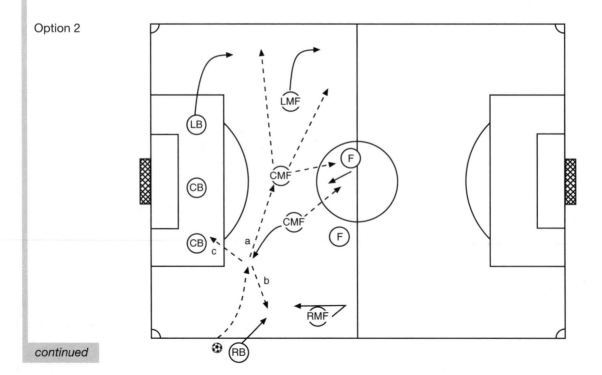

continued

Option 3

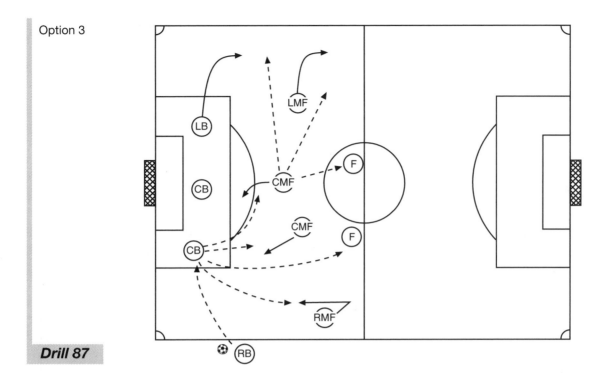

Drill 87

88 Long Throw-Ins From the Defensive Third

Purpose

To practice timing of runs to the ball and off the ball for effective, attacking, long throw-ins from the defensive third of the field, which will exploit a pressing defense and initiate a quick counterattack.

Organization

Full-field practice, using a 4-4-2 system

Procedure

1. Set balls down just outside both touch lines. Direct a throw-in from a specific location, forcing the team to make some quick decisions and some quick adjustments in positioning.

2. Rehearse option 1. Throw to the forward. The outside midfielder checks to the thrower along the touch line. The center back stays behind the ball to support the thrower. The central midfielder also checks to the thrower. One forward breaks to the corner flag, and one bends away. The thrower should throw over the checking flank midfielder to the forward breaking to the corner. The receiving forward should serve early to the second forward breaking to the goal on the counterattack.

3. Rehearse option 2. Throw to the central midfielder. The outside midfielder checks to the thrower along the touch line. The center back stays behind the ball to support the thrower. Both central midfielders check to the ball, and the farthest central midfielder should receive the throw from the outside back. One forward breaks to the corner flag, and one bends away. The throw should go over the closest checking central midfielder to the second central midfielder, who should play early to one of the forwards running to the goal or relieve the pressure by switching the point of attack to the opposite flank midfielder.

continued

Option 1

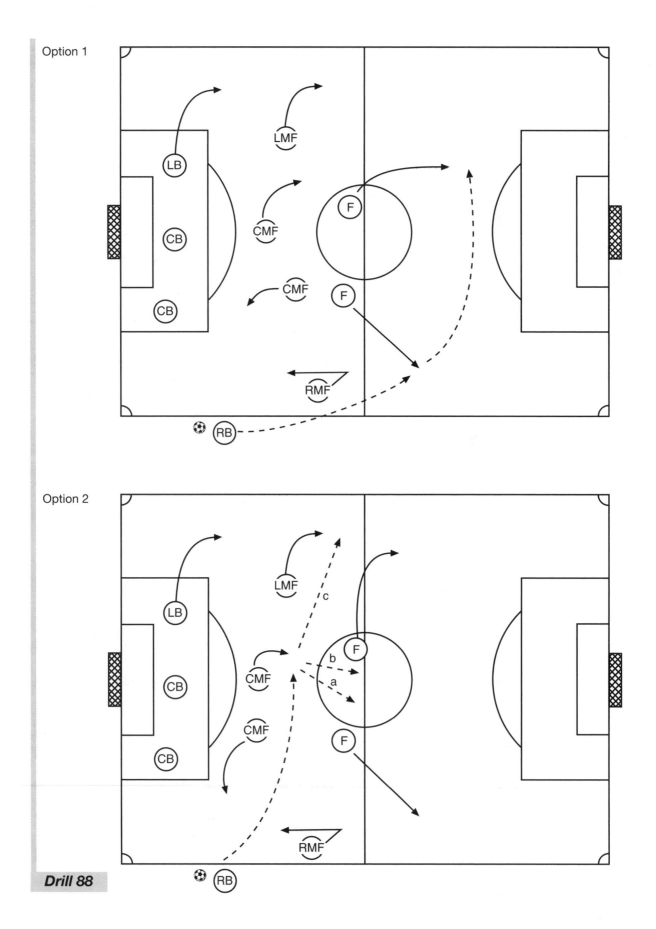

Option 2

Drill 88

89 Inswinging Corner Kick Rehearsals

Purpose

To practice inswinging serves for corner kicks along with the proper timing of runs to the ball and off the ball for effective, dangerous attacking corner kicks.

Organization

Half-field practice, using a 4-4-2 system

Procedure

1. Rehearse the same play and target different areas, for example, the near post or far post.

2. Practice both inswinging and outswinging kicks, forcing the team to make some quick decisions and some quick adjustments in positioning.

3. In a controlled scrimmage, call for a corner kick from any area of the field, forcing both the attacking and defending teams to react immediately and make quick tactical decisions.

4. Rehearse the inswinging corner. X_1, X_2, X_3, and X_4 are stationed near the penalty spot. X_5 is in the goal area, and X_6 is in the penalty arc at the D. X_7 should be at approximately the 30- or 35-yard line in position to play a defensive clearance back into the penalty area. X_8 and X_9 should remain at about midfield to prevent any counters.

X_1 would break toward the D, so X_1 and X_6 would control the third six-yard box (from the penalty spot to the edge of the penalty area). X_5 would break to the near post, X_2 would follow the vacated space to the center of the goal, and X_4 would bend away to the far post. X_3 would also bend away, attempting to cover the second third and any ball served all the way across. The server would most likely try to find X_5, X_2, or X_4.

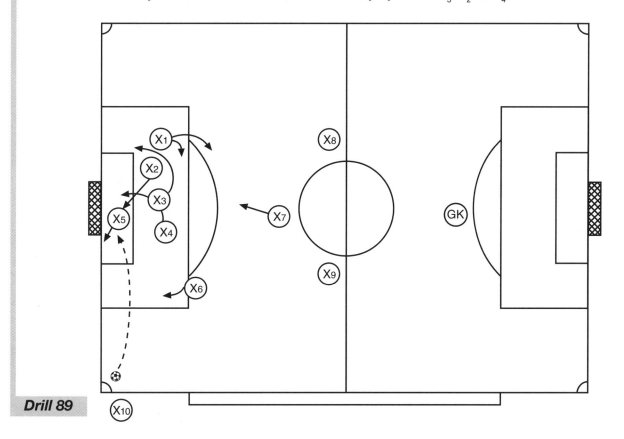

Drill 89

90 Outswinging Corner Kick Rehearsals

Purpose

To practice outswinging corner kick serves along with the proper timing of runs to the ball and off the ball for effective, dangerous attacking corner kicks.

Organization

Half-field practice, using a 4-4-2 system

Procedure

1. Rehearse the same play and target different areas, for example, the near post or far post.

2. Practice both inswinging and outswinging kicks, forcing the team to make some quick decisions and some quick adjustments in positioning.

3. In a controlled scrimmage, call for a corner kick from any area of the field, forcing both the attacking and defending teams to react immediately and make quick tactical decisions.

4. Rehearse the outswinging corner. X_1, X_2, X_3, and X_4 are stationed near the penalty spot. X_5 is in the goal area, and X_6 is in the penalty arc or the D. X_7 should be at approximately the 30- or 35-yard line in position to play a defensive clearance back into the penalty area. X_8 and X_9 should remain at about midfield to prevent any counters.

X_1 would break toward the D, so X_1 and X_6 would control the third six-yard box (from the penalty spot to the edge of the penalty area). X_5 would bend to the far post, and X_2 would bend away, attempting to cover the second third and any ball served all the way across. X_4 would bend away to the far post, and X_3 would run to the near post. The server would most likely try to find X_2, X_3, or X_4.

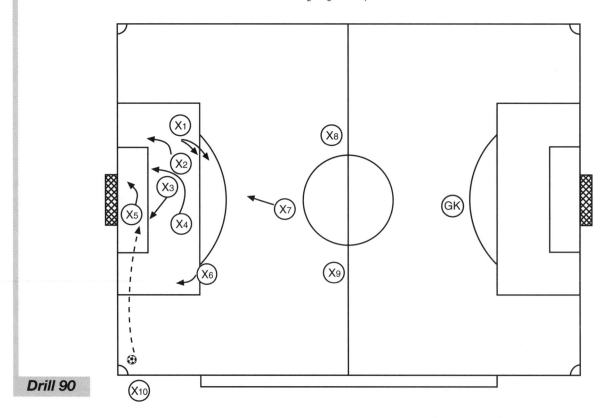

Drill 90

91 Short Corner Kick Rehearsals

Purpose

To practice short, quick corner kicks along with the proper timing of runs to the ball and off the ball for effective, dangerous attacking corner kicks.

Organization

Half-field practice, using a 4-4-2 system

Procedure

1. Rehearse the same play and target different areas, for example, the near post or far post.

2. Practice both inswinging and outswinging kicks, forcing the team to make some quick decisions and some quick adjustments in positioning.

3. In a controlled scrimmage, call for a corner kick from any area of the field, forcing both the attacking and defending teams to react immediately and make quick tactical decisions.

4. Rehearse the short corner kick. X_1, X_2, X_3, and X_4 are stationed near the penalty spot. X_5 is in the goal area, and X_6 is in the penalty arc or the D. X_7 should be at approximately the 30- or 35-yard line in position to play a defensive clearance back into the penalty area. X_8 and X_9 should remain at about midfield to prevent any counters.

X_7, X_6, or X_4 would break toward the server in the corner. X_1 would break toward midfield to take X_7's place in case of a breakdown and a counterattack. X_5 would go to the center of the goal, X_2 would bend to the far post, and X_3 would go to the near post. The server would play to X_4, X_6, or X_7. The receiver would then play immediately into the penalty area or perhaps back to the server, who could also serve into the area. Players not receiving the short ball from the corner should quickly get to a position to play the first or second ball served.

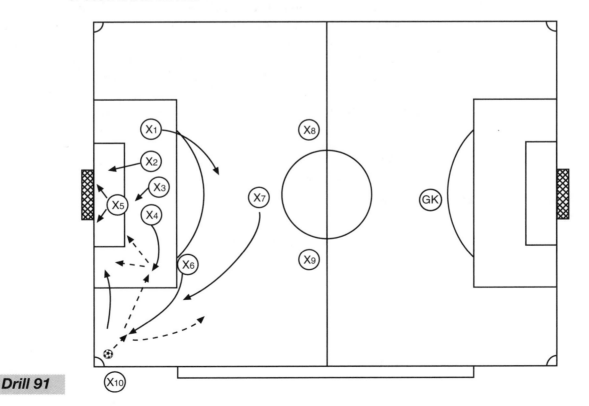

Drill 91

CHAPTER
10
Direct and Indirect Free Kicks

Sam Koch
University of Massachusetts

Over 33 percent of the goals scored in the 1998 World Cup in France were scored off restarts. In the championship game, France scored two of its three goals on direct free kicks. Of the last five goals that the University of Massachusetts scored in the 1998 season, four were on restarts. Because so many goals result from restarts, it makes sense to spend practice time on set plays. Yet how many coaches wait until the last day or two of preseason to start working on them?

What is the difference between a direct and an indirect free kick? A direct free kick is a free kick from which a goal can be scored directly against the penalized team. An indirect free kick is a free kick from which a goal cannot be scored unless the ball has been played (passed the distance of the circumference of the ball) and then touched by another player from either team before passing through the goal. The rules are straightforward. It is strategically helpful for your players to know what type of foul awards what type of free kick. The main fouls that award *direct* free kicks are

1. kicking or attempting to kick an opponent,
2. striking or attempting to strike an opponent,
3. tripping or attempting to trip an opponent,
4. a hand ball,
5. a hand ball by a goalkeeper outside the 18-yard box,
6. pushing or holding an opponent, and
7. a violent charge.

The most common fouls that result in *indirect* free kicks are

1. offsides,
2. illegal obstruction,

3. a goalkeeper carrying the ball more than four steps,

4. a goalkeeper taking more than five seconds to release the ball,

5. illegal substitution,

6. dissent by word or action with a referee's decision,

7. unsportsmanlike behavior, and

8. dangerous play.

Set plays can be highly successful for several reasons. First, the offensive team is without any immediate pressure because the defending team must be 10 yards from the ball until it is played. Second, the offensive team is playing a stationary ball, which is easier to strike than one that is moving, especially in trying to bend a shot around the wall. Third, the offensive team knows the plays and has had time to practice the patterns and timing of the runs with the timing of the service. Fourth, because a foul stops play, the offense has time to get all their top players involved. For example, defenders who are good headers have time to move forward into the penalty area to be on the offensive end of a driven ball. Because of the time allowed to move players forward, the offensive team can have as many as nine players in a concentrated area, which puts an extra burden on the defending team.

Observe three principles to achieve successful restarts:

1. Practice them efficiently and often.

2. Keep them simple.

3. Make sure the plays fit
   - your players' strengths,
   - the defenses you face,
   - the field conditions,
   - the weather, and
   - your location on the field.

For all free kicks players must understand the need to practice the plays. The timing of the runs is critical to the success of the set plays. The quality of the service is vital. If you cannot put the ball in the area you want, then it is going to be nearly impossible to get on the other end of the serve and put it in the back of the net.

Players need to practice these skills as individuals and as a team. Alone or in small groups, players can practice the technique of striking a bending ball around a wall or a driven ball to the near-post area. Practice as a team is also essential to putting together, as you would a puzzle, all the pieces of the play.

Teaching these individual and team techniques can be difficult. Coaches more often think about it than do it. During preseason, you should identify players who will be taking the set plays. Review, fine tune, and teach the techniques that players will need before they practice them on their own. Servers and strikers should spend an extra 15 minutes every practice perfecting their skills.

You can practice bending direct and indirect shots and services a number of ways. You can take shots or serve around an imaginary wall created in the mind; a skeleton wall marked out by two corner flags; a real wall made up of freshmen or rookies; or a professionally made or home-made portable wall, depending on your budget and your ability with a hammer and saw. If you make the wall yourself, make it light enough that one player can move it, sturdy enough to take the blow of a hard shot, and movable (wheels recommended).

The players who are targets of your services should practice the timing and patterns of their runs so defenders find it difficult to mark them. The bending run is hard to track and allows the offensive player more flexibility to get into good positions to head balls on goal. A key tactical point, often overlooked, is that players need to practice heading the ball down. It is almost impossible for a keeper to stop a ball that is headed down just inside the goal line.

Once players master their individual roles, you should practice restarts as a team to perfect the timing and location of the runs. You can do this in scrimmage situations. When the ball is in an area where you want to work on a restart, blow the whistle for "mystery fouls" and indicate direct or indirect kick. Do not call too many fouls or you will sacrifice the gamelike flow of the scrimmage. You can practice set plays for the offense as well as the defense against set pieces. Working restarts into a scrimmage is the most realistic way I know to practice them. You may choose another method of practicing set plays, but be sure that it is competitive.

Keep your restarts simple. If you want to have a chance to score on every play, you need to have a shot on net on each restart that you perform in a game. The fewer passes you make before you shoot, the more likely it is that you will get a shot off. The best set play is a direct shot on goal. If a foul occurs near the front of the goal just outside the penalty area and you have a player who can bend a ball over or around a wall, that is the only set play you need for that area of the field. If you do not have this special player, you need to come up with some other types of plays that will give you good opportunities to get a shot on goal.

When deciding what type of set plays to use, remember to keep them simple and fit them to your players' strengths. If you have three players who are animals in the air, it makes sense to use plays that serve balls in the air to the back post or midgoal area. If you have a gifted 1 vs. 1 attacking player, use plays that isolate him or her with one defender to beat. Always focus on getting a shot on goal. Keep your runs simple and your serves into the danger areas as direct as possible.

You want to attack the other team's weakness with your set plays. If you know that they are weak in the air and the goalkeeper does not come off his or her line, driving balls into the air just outside the six-yard box will cause all kinds of trouble. If you know that the team you are facing is slow setting up to defend restarts, you should practice putting the ball in play right away. This can create many good scoring chances if the entire offensive team is prepared. If the offensive team is not ready for the quick restart, it can be curtains because your team is vulnerable to the quick counterattack.

Know the locations on the field where your set pieces work the best. The clearest example is that some direct and indirect plays need space behind the wall to work. If the keeper's wall is set up 5 yards inside the 18-yard box, a chip over the wall will land in the keeper's hands most of the time. If you are taking the free kick from an area where the defense sets up the wall another 10 yards out from the goal, then the chip-over-the-wall play has a much better chance of working. The weather is another factor. You have to take into account the rain, the wind, and the conditions of the playing surface when you decide what plays to use. If you are playing a game in the steady rain and the field conditions are poor to begin with, a play that isolates a player one on one is not effective. A driven ball into the near-post area will cause more problems for the defense in these conditions.

Set plays will be an important part of your team's offense if you take advantage of your players' strengths and attack where your opponent is weak. As a coach you need to make sure that players work individually on their specialties and that your team practices the set-play patterns as a group. Game situations in practice will give your players opportunities to practice determining the best restart for the specific offense and defense on the field, the weather, and the location and condition of the restart area. I hope the collection of set plays that I have put together helps you design plays that will use your team's strengths. Good luck with your upcoming season.

92 BC

Organization

Players 1 and 2 line up on either side of the wall. Players 3, 4, 5, and 6 line up together on the far side of the penalty area. Players 7 and 8 line up on the ball, and players 9 and 10 hold at midfield for defensive cover.

Procedure

1. Players 1 and 2 start the play by running toward players 3, 4, 5, and 6, pulling two defenders with them. Player 7 runs over the ball, bending his or her run outside the wall. Player 8 serves the ball outside the wall to player 7, who

   • dribbles and shoots,

   • shoots with his or her first touch, or

   • crosses the ball to the back-post area for players 1, 4, 5, and 6.

2. Player 3 drops back to help defend just before player 8 serves the ball. Player 2 holds at the D to keep a defender out of the area and collect any ball that rebounds into this area.

3. After player 8 has served the ball, players 4, 5, and 6 time their runs to the back-post area for the back-post service or any loose ball that comes free to this area.

Variation

Player 7 can dribble all the way to the end line and drive the ball on the ground back between the 6-yard box and the penalty stripe for players 1 and 2. Players 1 and 2 delay their runs so they arrive in this area just as the ball arrives.

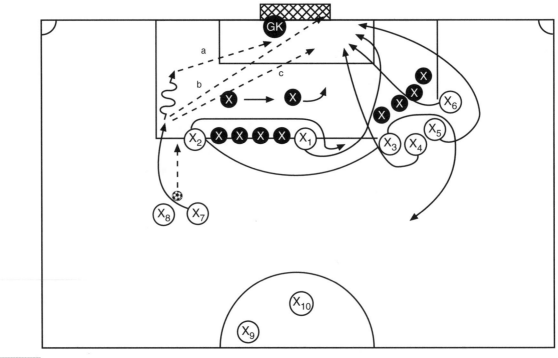

Drill 92

93 Pickhardt

Organization

Players 1, 2, and 3 line up around the ball. Players 4, 5, and 6 line up outside the 18-yard box on the far-post side. Player 7 lines up inside the wall. Players 8, 9, and 10 hold to prevent a counterattack if possession is lost.

Procedure

1. Player 3 runs over the ball and into the last player on the outside of the wall, stops, turns, and starts yelling at players 2 and 1 about how player 1 should have made a run to the inside and that player 2 was supposed to serve it. Player 3 is doing this as he or she walks back toward the ball.

2. When player 3 gets two-thirds of the way back to the ball, player 2 flicks the ball with his or her foot over the wall for player 7, who runs on to it and

   • shoots on goal or

   • slips the ball into the path of players 4, 5, or 6 if they are in alone.

Variations

• If the defense covers the area behind the wall with an extra defender, player 1 should line up on the outside of the wall and then run to the outside of the 18-yard box to pull the defender away.

• Player 9 times his or her run from a deep defensive position to come in late as an additional shooter just square of the wall. The player starts his or her run by walking up to the ball while 3 is doing his or her acting job. If 3 is good, no one will see 9 coming forward. Player 9 now adds the option of a square pass from player 2 if the defending team has a player covering the area behind the wall for the flick.

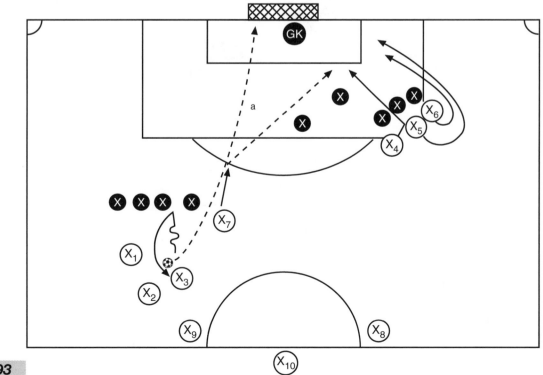

94 Wall Pass

Organization

Players 1 and 2 line up on the ball. Players 3, 4, 5, and 6 line up at the far-post corner of the 18-yard box. Player 7 lines up outside the wall. Players 8, 9, and 10 line up in defensive positions near midfield.

Procedure

1. Players 3, 4, and 5 start running diagonally away from the defensive wall. Player 6 uses runs by players 3, 4, and 5 to make it tough for the defensive mark to track his or her run. Player 6 runs at the defensive wall, setting up a wall pass from player 1.

2. Player 7 runs behind the wall across the 18-yard box toward players 3, 4, and 5, pulling the defensive cover away from the space behind the wall. Player 2 starts a run to the outside of the wall once player 6 has broken free of other runners.

3. Player 1 passes the ball to player 6, who first times the ball behind the wall for player 2. Player 2 then

   • passes the ball to players 3, 4, or 5, who have broken free of their marks;

   • dribbles toward the six-yard box to commit the goalkeeper, then passes the ball to player 3, 4, or 5 running in;

   • shoots with his or her first touch; or

   • dribbles and shoots on goal.

Variations

• Player 1 fakes a pass to player 6 and chips the ball into space behind the defenders for players 3, 4, and 5 to run on to. This is an effective option if defenders do not track player 7's run.

• Player 1 knocks the ball square to player 10, who is running up from a defensive position to crack a long shot.

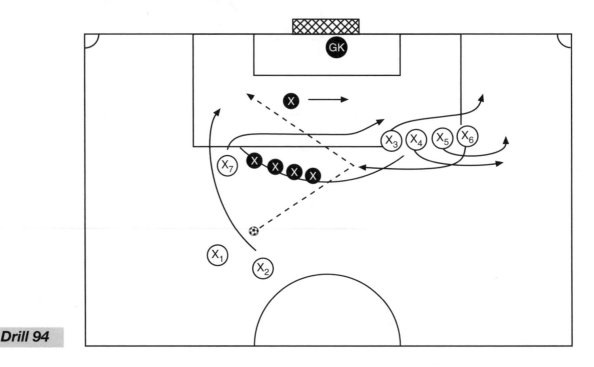

Drill 94

95 Argentina

Organization

Players 1, 2, and 3 line up around the ball. Player 4 sets up inside the wall. Players 5 and 6 position themselves on the corner of the 18-yard box. Players 7 and 8 line up on the near-post corner of the 18-yard box. Players 9 and 10 hold at midfield to defend.

Procedure

1. Player 3 makes a run toward the wall and cuts to the right toward players 5 and 6. Player 3's run pulls a defender away from the covering position behind the wall.

2. Player 2 runs over the ball toward players 7 and 8, pulling the left defender away from a covering position behind the wall.

3. Players 7 and 8 start runs 5 yards to the outside of the 18-yard box. Player 7 holds, and player 8 drops back to defend.

4. Player 4, just after player 2 runs over the ball, breaks away from the wall. Player 1 serves the ball to player 4's feet. Player 4 collects, turns, and shoots on goal.

Variations

If player 4 is closed down and cannot shoot, he or she can

- pass back to player 1 to shoot,
- pass to players 2 and 7 on the left side of the wall for a shot, or
- pass the ball to players 3, 5, and 6 on the right side of the wall for a shot.

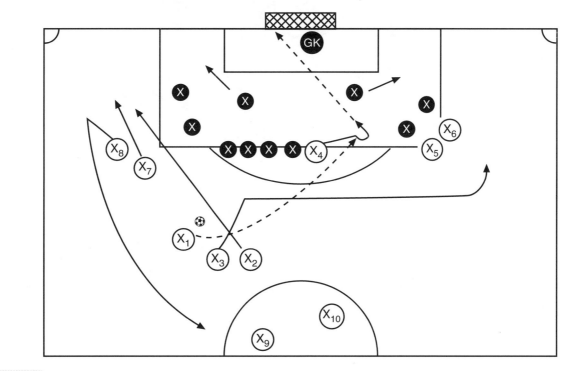

Drill 95

96 Rope

Organization

Player 1 lines up next to the ball on the flank. Players 2, 3, 4, and 5 line up on the 6-yard box even with the ball. Players 6 and 7 line up at the corner of the penalty area. Players 8, 9, and 10 are in defensive positions near midfield.

Procedure

1. Player 1 gives a signal for players 2 through 7 to start their runs away from the ball. Player 1 serves the ball to the near-post area when players 2, 3, 4, and 5 reach the edge of the six-yard box.

2. Player 5 times a run so he or she is the first player through and flicks or dummies the ball through for players 2, 3, 4, or 6 to head on goal. Player 2 runs to the near post, player 3 runs to the midgoal area, and player 4 runs to the back post. Player 6 runs from the edge of the penalty area, bending the run so that he or she arrives in the back-post area for the ball if it makes it past the other players.

3. Player 7 checks away from the ball when player 1 gives the signal and then cuts back to the penalty area for any ball that pops out. Player 8 moves forward to be in position to shoot on goal if a ball bounces free around the penalty area.

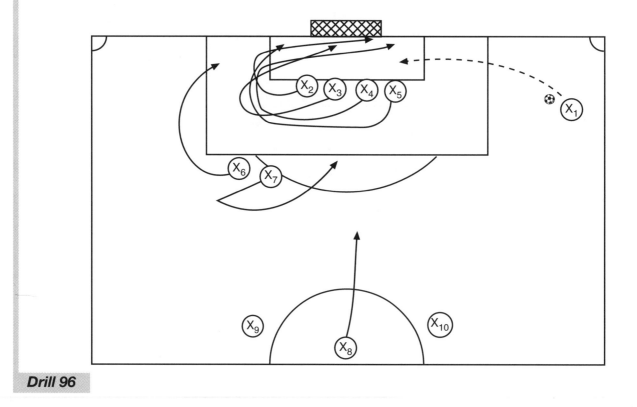

Drill 96

97 Garcia

Organization

Player 1 lines up on the ball. Player 2 is standing about 2 yards away, facing the ball. Player 3 is about 5 yards behind the ball facing the goal. Player 5 is on the inside of the wall. Player 4 lines up on the right corner of the 18-yard box. Players 6 and 7 line up on the left corner of the penalty box. Player 8 is 10 to 15 yards behind player 3. Players 9 and 10 line up in a defensive position near the center circle.

Procedure

1. Player 1 passes the ball to player 2, and player 3 starts a run toward the spot one foot from player 2's feet. Player 2 stops the ball on the spot for player 3 to strike on the goal.

2. If a defender rushes the ball from a position at the corner of the wall, player 2 pulls the ball back away from the rushing defender and touches the ball to the side just enough so he or she can take one step and shoot the ball past the goalkeeper.

Variations

Player 3 can chip the ball for player 4, who is breaking toward the goal just outside the 18-yard box. Player 4 then shoots on the keeper, chips the keeper, or heads the ball back to the penalty-kick spot to players 5, 6, and 7, who have run into these predetermined areas.

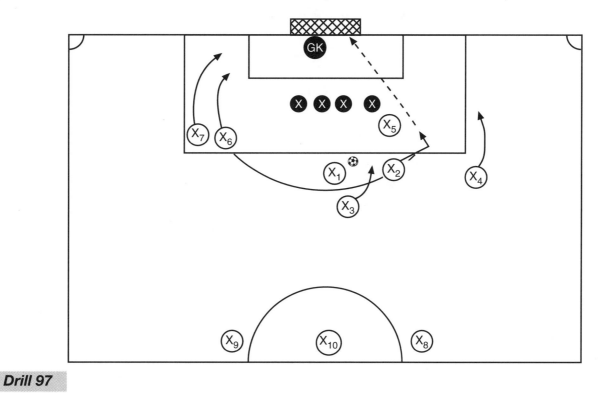

Drill 97

98 Butler

Organization

Player 1 lines up on the ball, and player 3 lines up 5 to 7 yards from the corner of the 18-yard box on the 18-yard line. Players 2, 4, 5, and 6 line up near the opposite corner of the 18-yard box. Player 7 lines up 15 yards outside the center circle. Players 8, 9, and 10 are near midfield in defensive positions.

Procedure

1. Player 3 runs over to players 2, 4, 5, and 6. Player 2 runs around players 4, 5, and 6 and sprints across the front of the 18-yard box.

2. Player 1 passes the ball on the ground to player 2's feet. Player 2 turns and takes on the isolated defender. Player 2 then either shoots, beats the defender on the dribble and shoots, or beats the defender and takes the ball to the end line and slots it across the goal mouth for player 3, 4, 5, or 6.

3. Player 7 moves forward toward the penalty area to be ready to clean up any ball that pops free in that area.

Variations

• If two defenders cover player 2, player 1 chips the ball to the back-post area where the defense is not as strong.

• Player 1 slips player 7 the ball. Player 7 takes the ball to the goal and either chips it to the back-post area for players 3, 4, 5, and 6 or passes it to player 2, who has broken free from his or her defender.

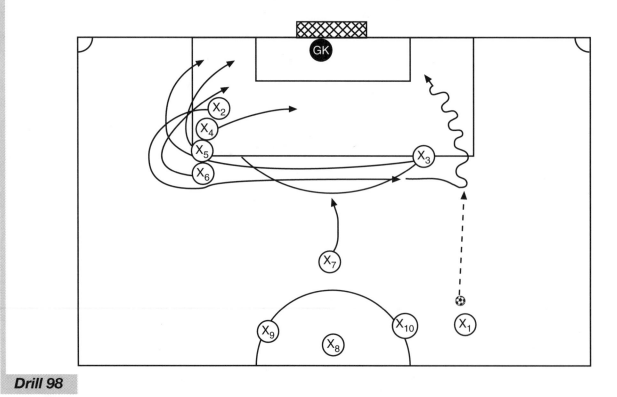

99 Cleveland

Organization

Player 1 is on the ball near midfield. Players 2 through 7 set up together on the top of the penalty area. Player 8 is 10 to 15 yards behind players 2 through 7. Players 9 and 10 are in defensive positions at midfield.

Procedure

1. Player 1 serves the ball to the top of the penalty area for player 3 or 2 to flick on to one of the shaded areas A or B, which are marked on the diagram.

2. Players 6 and 4 bend their runs to attack shaded area A. Players 5 and 7 bend their runs to attack shaded area B.

3. Player 8 holds position to collect any poor defensive clearance and serve the ball to the feet of players 5 and 7 or players 4 and 6.

Variation

Player 1 makes a short pass to player 10, who dribbles until confronted and then chips the ball to the back-post area.

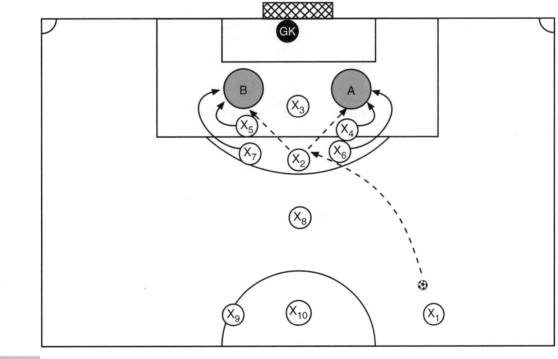

Drill 99

100 Toledo

Organization

The setup is similar to Cleveland's setup. Player 1 sets up standing next to the ball. Players 2, 3, and 4 line up on top of the penalty area. Players 5, 6, 7, and 8 are outside the 18-yard box and back about 10 to 15 yards. Players 9 and 10 are in defensive positions at midfield.

Procedure

1. Player 1 serves the ball in the air to players 2, 3, and 4 at the top of the penalty area.

2. The player who gets under the ball flicks it to zone A or B.

3. Players 5 and 6 time their runs into zone A and players 7 and 8 into zone B to arrive simultaneously with the ball for a one-touch shot.

Variations

If the flick from player 2, 3, or 4 is hard to handle, the player who gets to the ball can serve it across to one of the players running into the other zoned area for a shot. Another option is to play it back to the feet of player 2, 3, or 4 for a shot.

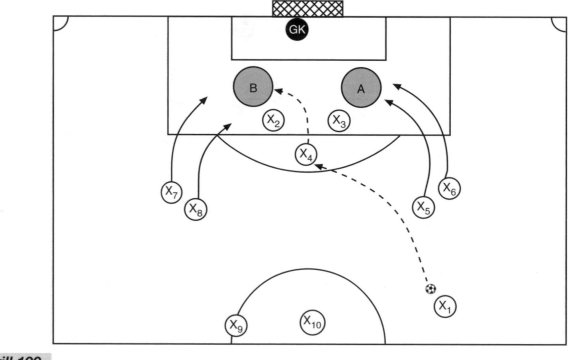

Drill 100

101 Defender's Choice

Organization

Player 1 sets up next to the ball. Players 2, 3, 4, and 5 line up on the back side of the 18-yard box. Players 7 and 6 set up about 15 to 20 yards back of the 18-yard box, one even with each of its corners. Player 8 lines up between the penalty area and the midfield stripe. Players 9 and 10 line up in defensive positions at midfield.

Procedure

1. Player 1 drops his or her head and starts the approach to serve the ball into the six-yard box. Player 2 bends a run to the near post, players 3 and 4 to the central goal area, and player 5 to the back post.

2. Players 9 and 10 move to the right side of the central circle. Player 1 steps over the ball. Players 2, 3, 4, and 5 keep running—players 2 and 3 all the way to midfield, player 4 to the edge of the center circle, and player 5 curling to the top of the penalty area. Player 6 drops back to midfield. Players 8 and 7 move 10 to 15 yards closer to the 18-yard box.

3. Now player 1 steps back and serves the ball into the box. Meanwhile player 7 runs to the near post, player 8 runs to the middle of the 6-yard box, and players 9 and 10 run to the back post.

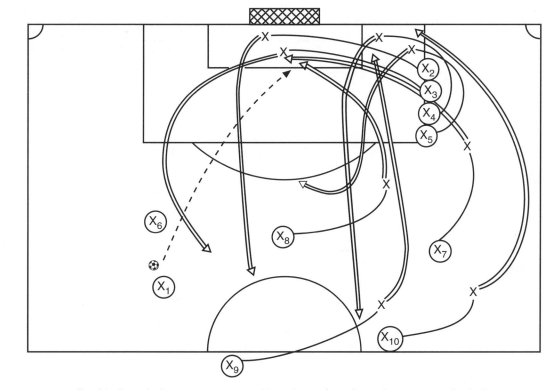

Double lines indicate movement taking place after player 1 steps over the ball.

Drill 101

102 Nixon

Organization

Player 1 sets up next to the ball. Players 2, 3, 4, 5, and 6 line up on the edge of the 18-yard box. Players 7 and 8 set up 20 yards behind the penalty area. Players 9 and 10 take defensive positions at midfield.

Procedure

1. Player 2 runs to the near post, player 3 runs to the middle of the 6-yard box closer to the near post, player 4 runs to the middle of the 6-yard box closer to the back post, and player 6 runs to the back post.

2. Player 5 doubles back and around to a defensive position, bending the run away from the central part of the penalty box. Players 7 and 8 run to the top of the penalty area. Player 1 serves the ball for them to volley on goal.

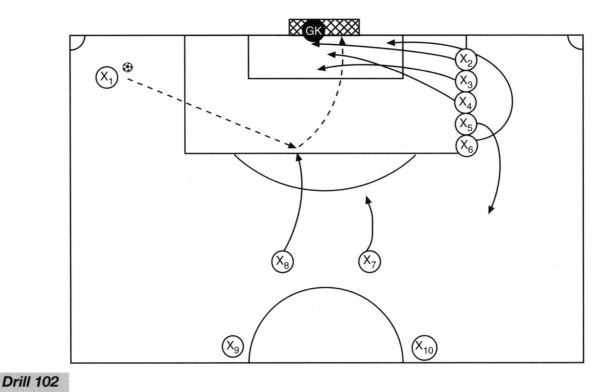

Drill 102

103 Leeson

Organization

Player 1 lines up next to the ball. Player 3 lines up square to the ball 3 yards away. Player 2 lines up between players 1 and 3 about five yards behind. Player 4 is about 5 yards farther to the right of player 3 and 15 yards behind. Player 5 stands on the far side of the penalty area, away from the defensive wall. Players 6 and 7 stand at the corner of the 18-yard box near player 5. Players 8 and 10 hold at midfield.

Procedure

1. Player 1 passes the ball to player 3, who stops the ball with the sole of his or her foot. Player 2 starts the approach to the ball and fakes the shot. Player 5 runs toward the front of the defensive wall to try to pull away a defender and block the goalkeeper's view of the ball. Player 6 checks his or her run to the right and then cuts in front of the defender to run into the 18-yard box for any knock down. Player 7 bends his or her run around the defender and rushes into the 18-yard box for any knock down that rebounds into that area.

2. When player 1 passes the ball to player 3, player 4, acting as if he or she is not in the play by pretending to be in a conversation with players 7, 8, and 10, turns and sprints toward the penalty area. Player 3 heels the ball square into the path of player 4, who shoots on goal.

Variations

- Player 4 can pass the ball to player 6 after player 5 has pulled the defender out of covering position.

- Player 4 can chip the ball into the space behind for player 7 to run on to, shoot, or pass back in front of the goal for players 6, 5, and 1. Player 1 has made a run around the outside of the wall after the original pass to player 3.

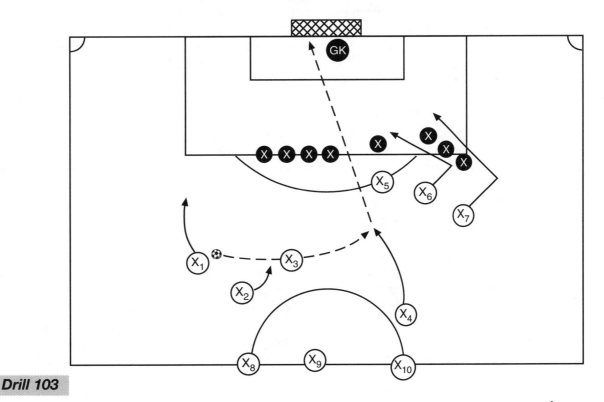

Drill 103

PART IV

Developing Individual Attacking Skills

Parts I, II, and III have dealt with the tactical side of attacking soccer—the methods, movement patterns, and strategies essential to scoring goals. Tactics provide a frame of reference for the myriad decisions players make during each game. Knowing what to do and when to do it, however, is only two-thirds of the equation. Players must develop the skills that physically enable them to do it. For example, although a player may understand the various passing combinations used to advance the ball through the middle third of the field, such knowledge is of little benefit if he or she lacks the ability to pass and receive the ball effectively under the pressures of game competition.

Part IV focuses on the technical skills that each player must master to contribute to the team attack. These are the nuts and bolts of attacking soccer—fundamental elements of play that enable players to fulfill their responsibilities on an individual, group, and team level. Passing, receiving, and dribbling skills are used to possess the ball, penetrate opposing defenses, and create scoring opportunities. Heading and shooting skills are used to finish a successful attack.

Chapter 11 provides a series of drills designed to improve players' ability to pass and receive the ball. Passing and receiving skills form the thread that bonds 11 individuals into a smooth-functioning unit, enabling teammates to play in combination with one another. These essential skills are linked to one another in the sense that each ball passed should, at least in theory, be received and controlled by another player. Mastery of the various passing and receiving skills is a must for all field players.

Chapter 12 focuses on the development of dribbling skills. The ability to take on and beat an opponent on the dribble is characteristic of all top-flight attacking players. Dribbling in soccer can to some degree be equated to dribbling in basketball. Players dribble to advance the ball into open space, to penetrate opposing defenses, to commit defenders, and to maintain possession of the ball when under immediate challenge from an opponent. Although styles may vary from one player to another, the most successful dribblers incorporate several common elements into their technique. These include body feints, sudden changes of speed and direction, deceptive foot movements, and close control of the ball.

Chapter 13 focuses on heading skills, a topic too often neglected during training sessions. Soccer is the only major sport in which players use their heads to propel the ball. Some teams, depending upon their style of play, rely on heading skills more than others. Norway and Mexico are cases in point. The Norwegians tend to play a direct style of play, serving long balls to their forwards, who are expected to challenge for and win their share of air balls. In contrast to Norway, the Mexicans play the ball primarily along the ground with an emphasis on foot speed and technical proficiency. Regardless, it is inevitable that the soccer ball will be in the air for a good portion of every game. As a consequence, all field players should develop adequate heading skills.

Chapter 14 addresses the most difficult task in soccer—finishing the attack with a goal scored. Success as a goal scorer depends on a number of factors. Qualities such as anticipation, determination, and composure under pressure are important, as is the ability to strike the ball with accuracy and power. All field players must develop proficiency at striking balls that are rolling, bouncing, or dropping from above. They must be able to execute shooting skills under the game pressures of restricted space, limited time, physical fatigue, and determined opponents challenging for the ball. The drills in chapter 14 are designed to achieve that aim.

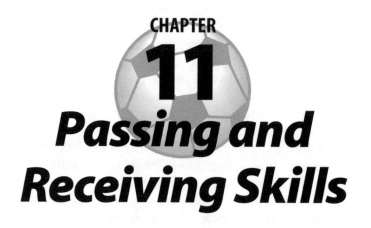

11
Passing and Receiving Skills

Joe Luxbacher
University of Pittsburgh

Passing and receiving skills provide the thread that connects the individual parts of a team, the players, into a smoothly functioning whole. The ability to pass the ball accurately and with proper pace is essential to successful attacking combinations. Equally important is the ability to receive and control passes from teammates. A player's first touch of the ball is the most critical one because it can create time for decision making and space for skill execution. The player who feels the pressure and controls the ball into space away from a challenging opponent gains precious moments and additional space in which to choose and execute his or her next movement. On the other hand, the player who fails to recognize pressure and whose first touch on the ball places him or her under immediate challenge from an opponent will be at a decided disadvantage.

Whenever possible, players should pass the ball along the ground rather than through the air. Ground passes can be played with greater accuracy than lofted passes and are also easier for teammates to control. Three passing skills are commonly used to pass the ball along the ground—inside-of-the-foot, outside-of-the-foot, and instep. The choice of technique depends on the situation. Players most often receive and control ground passes using either the inside or outside surfaces of the foot.

Despite the shortcomings of passing the ball through the air, situations do occur that dictate use of lofted passes. For example, an opponent may be blocking a passing lane between two attacking teammates. The only way to get the ball from one attacker to the other is to chip it over the opponent. Field players must become adept at playing the ball accurately through the air over varying distances. On the flip side of the coin, all players must develop the ability to receive and control balls directly out of the air. The most common receiving surfaces players use to control balls dropping from above are the instep, thigh, and chest.

The following drills are appropriate for practicing all types of passing and receiving techniques. You can modify each drill to emphasize specific passing or receiving skills.

104 Complete the Circuit

Purpose

To develop passing and receiving skills.

Organization

Use markers to outline a playing area of 25 by 40 yards. Station six to eight players within the area. Number the players, beginning with 1 and continuing up through the number of players in the group. Three balls are required.

Procedure

1. Each of three players has possession of a ball to begin.

2. All players begin moving within the area. Those with a ball dribble, and those without a ball jog.

3. Each dribbler locates the player with the next greater number and passes to him or her (that is, player 1 passes to player 2, player 4 to player 5, and so on). The player with the highest number passes to player 1 to complete the circuit.

4. All players move continuously for the duration of the drill, passing to the player numbered directly above them and receiving passes from the player numbered directly below them.

5. Play for 10 to 15 minutes.

Key Points

- Encourage players to pass and receive the ball in a smooth, controlled manner.

- Emphasize accuracy and correct pace of passes.

- Players should not stop the ball as they receive it; rather, they should control the ball in the direction of their next movement.

Variations

- Impose restrictions on players (for example, pass with weakest foot only, pass with outside-of-the-foot technique only).

- Increase the number of balls per group.

- Add a defender to the drill who attempts to intercept passes.

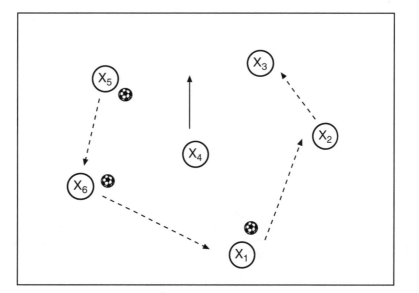

Drill 104

105 Hunter-Fox

Purpose

To improve passing skills and to develop agility and mobility.

Organization

Use markers to outline an area of 25 yards square. Designate three players as hunters. Place the hunters, each with a ball, outside the area. All other players are foxes and take positions inside the area (without soccer balls). Position an ample supply of soccer balls (at least one for each player in the drill) just outside the playing area.

Procedure

1. On the coach's command the hunters dribble into the area, and each attempts to pass his or her ball to contact a fox below the knees.

2. Foxes may move anywhere within the area to avoid being hit with a ball.

3. A player contacted by a passed ball leaves the area, collects a ball, and reenters the game as a hunter.

4. A hunter who passes his or her ball to contact a fox becomes a fox.

5. Play for 10 to 15 minutes.

Key Points

- Encourage hunters to dribble close to their targets before passing the ball.
- Require hunters to keep their passes low (below the target's knees).

Variations

- Adjust the area size to accommodate the ages and abilities of players.
- Impose restrictions to emphasize a particular type of pass (for example, inside-of-the-foot passes only, passes with weakest foot only).

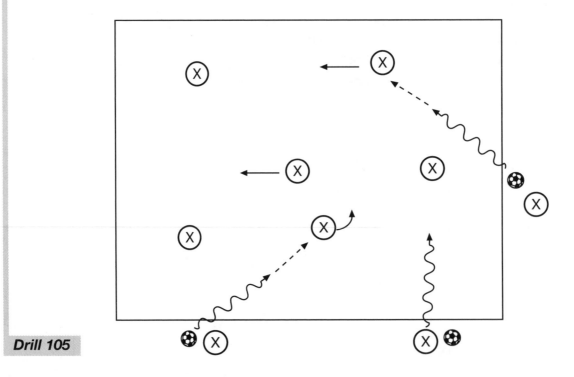

106 Hot Potato

Purpose

Group activity to develop ability to maintain possession of the ball through combination passing.

Organization

Use markers to outline an area of 20 yards square. Position seven players within the area; designate five as attackers and two as defenders. One attacker has possession of the ball to begin.

Procedure

1. Five attackers try to keep the ball from two defenders.
2. Limit attackers to three or fewer touches to pass and receive the ball.
3. A defender who intercepts a pass immediately becomes an attacker; the player who lost the ball becomes a defender.
4. Score one point for eight or more consecutive passes.
5. Play for 15 to 20 minutes.

Key Points

- Encourage players not to be caught with the hot potato. Emphasize quick ball movement.
- Players should take positions at wide angles of support.
- Emphasize the importance of the first touch when receiving the ball; encourage players to receive the ball into space away from the challenging defender.

Variation

Reduce the playing area or place restrictions on attackers (for example, two-touch passing only) to make the game more challenging.

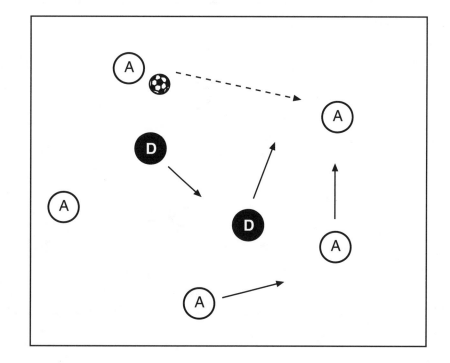

Drill 106

107 Toss and Receive to Score

Purpose

To develop ability to receive and control balls out of the air and to develop off-the-ball support movement.

Organization

Use markers to outline a playing area of 40 by 50 yards. Organize two equal teams of six to eight players each. Each team defends an end line of the field. Award one team possession of the ball.

Procedure

1. The team with the ball plays keep away from opponents.
2. Passing is accomplished by throwing (rather than kicking) the ball.
3. Players must receive and control the ball using their instep, thigh, or chest, and then catch the ball with their hands before it drops to the ground.
4. Players are permitted a maximum of four steps while in possession of the ball before passing it to a teammate.
5. The defending team gains possession by intercepting an opponent's pass or when an opponent fails to control the ball before it drops to the ground.
6. Defending players *are not* permitted to wrestle the ball away from opponents.
7. Award a team one point for 10 consecutive passes without loss of possession; award two points for completing a pass to a teammate positioned beyond the opponent's end line.
8. Play for 20 minutes; the team scoring the most points wins.

Key Points

- Attacking players must constantly move to support the teammate with the ball.

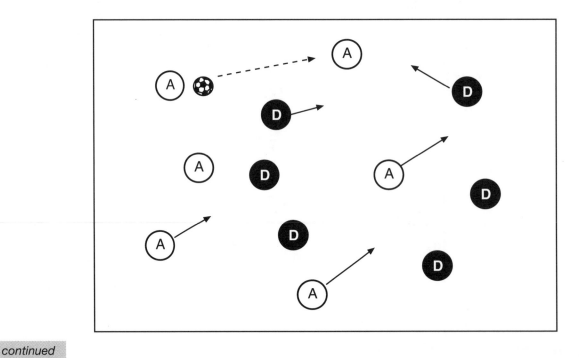

continued

- Encourage players to cushion the impact as they receive the ball by withdrawing the receiving surface as the ball arrives, creating a soft target.
- Encourage short, high-percentage passes rather than long tosses with little or no chance of completion.

Variations

- Add two neutral players to the drill who join the team in possession to create a numbers-up advantage for the attack.
- Place a full-size goal on the midpoint of each end line. To score, players must volley or half-volley a teammate's pass into the goal.

Drill 107

108 Game With Targets

Purpose

To develop passing and receiving skills, improve team play, and improve off-the-ball running patterns.

Organization

Play on a 40-by-60-yard field. Divide players into two equal teams of five to eight players each. Designate one player on each team as the target player. The target player should wear a distinct vest or shirt to differentiate him or her from teammates. Award one team possession of the ball to begin.

Procedure

1. Begin with a kickoff from the center of the field.
2. Objectives are twofold: to keep the ball from opponents and to complete passes to the target player.
3. Award one point for six consecutive passes without loss of possession; award two points for a pass completed to the target player.
4. Change of possession occurs when a defending player steals the ball, when the ball leaves the playing area, or after a point has been scored.
5. Regular soccer rules apply except for the method of scoring.
6. Play for 20 minutes.
7. The team scoring the most points wins.

Key Points

- Players must work in combination to keep the ball from opponents.
- Targets must position themselves to be available for passes from teammates.

Variations

- Reduce size of the playing area for advanced players.
- Designate two targets on each team.
- Impose restrictions on players (for example, limit the number of touches permitted to receive, control, and pass the ball).

continued

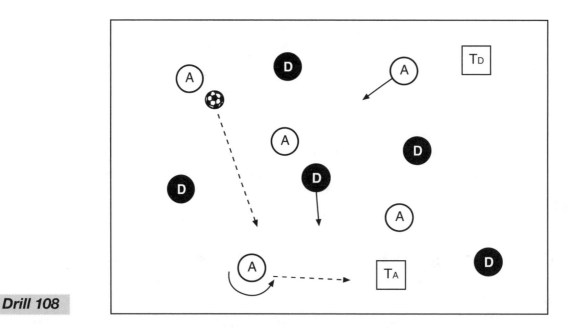

Drill 108

109 Perimeter Passing and Receiving

Purpose

To improve passing and receiving skills, to develop proper team shape (support movement), and to develop off-the-ball running patterns.

Organization

Use markers to outline an area of 25 by 40 yards. Organize three teams of three players each; station one team (defenders) in the center of the field. The remaining six players (attackers) take positions along the perimeter lines of the area.

Procedure

1. Attackers attempt to keep the ball from the defenders.
2. Attackers may move along the perimeter lines but may not enter the area to receive passes.
3. Limit touches to three or fewer to receive, control, and pass the ball.
4. When a defending player steals the ball his or her team immediately switches to the attack; the team that lost possession becomes the defending team.
5. Play continuously for 25 minutes.

Key Point

Encourage attackers to change the point of attack (location of the ball) quickly to unbalance the defending team.

Variations

- Adjust area size to accommodate the age and experience of players (for example, reducing the area size makes it more difficult for the attackers to maintain possession from defenders).
- Impose a limit of two or fewer touches to control and pass the ball.

continued

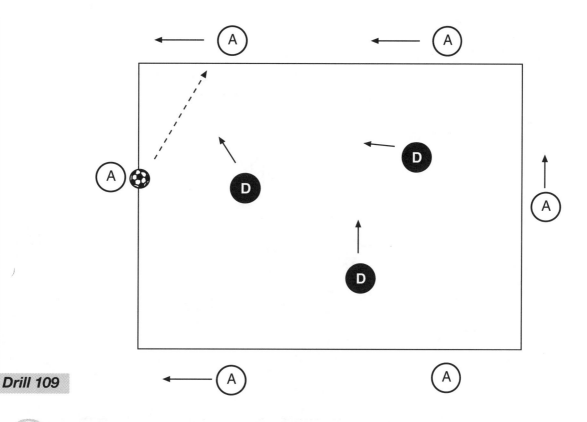

Drill 109

110 Numbers-Up Passing and Receiving

Purpose

To practice passing and receiving skills in game-simulated conditions.

Organization

Use markers to outline a field area of 20 by 30 yards. Position a goal 5 yards wide at the midpoint of each end line. Organize two teams of two players each. Designate two additional neutral players, who join the team in possession of the ball to create a 4 vs. 2 advantage for the attack. Award one team possession to begin.

Procedure

1. Each team defends a goal and can score in the opponent's goal.

2. Neutral players join the attacking team to create a 4 vs. 2 advantage for the attack.

3. Do not use goalkeepers.

4. Limit attacking players (plus neutrals) to three or fewer touches to receive, control, and pass or shoot the ball.

5. Score one point for a ball kicked through the opponent's goal below waist height.

Key Points

- Attacking players should use quick ball movement to unbalance outnumbered defenders.

- Encourage immediate transition to attack on change of possession.

- Emphasize proper attacking shape—width and depth (support).

continued

Variations

- Reduce area size for advanced players.
- Limit attacking players to two touches for passing and receiving.
- Position two small goals on each end line to provide additional scoring options.

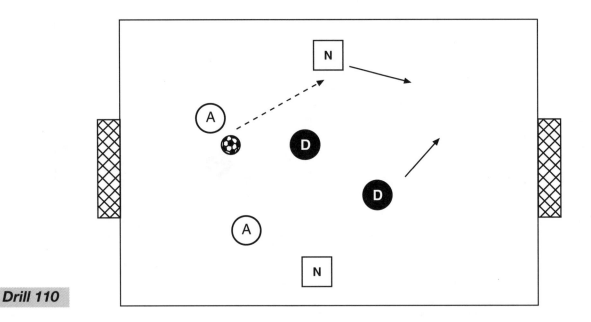

Drill 110

111 3 vs. 3 (Plus 4 Outside Grid) Possession Game

Purpose

To maintain possession of the ball from outnumbered opponents.

Organization

Use markers to outline an area of 20 by 30 yards. Organize two teams of three players each. Designate four additional players as neutrals. One neutral takes a position on each sideline and end line. Award one three-player team possession of the ball to begin.

Procedure

1. Neutrals join the team in possession to keep the ball from the defending team.
2. Neutrals may not enter the playing field; they must move along the sidelines and end lines of the field and are limited to three touches to control and pass the ball.
3. Neutrals may not pass to one another; they must receive the ball from and pass the ball to players competing within the field area.
4. If a defending player steals the ball, his or her team immediately becomes the attacking team and tries to maintain possession from their opponents.
5. Award a team one point for eight consecutive passes.
6. Play for 20 minutes.
7. The team scoring the most points wins.

continued

Key Points

- Encourage attackers to change the location of the ball (point of attack) constantly to prevent opponents from closing down space and time.
- Attacking players should constantly move in relation to movement of the ball to make themselves available for passes.

Variations

- Restrict neutral players to two touches.
- Adjust field area size to accommodate the ability of players.

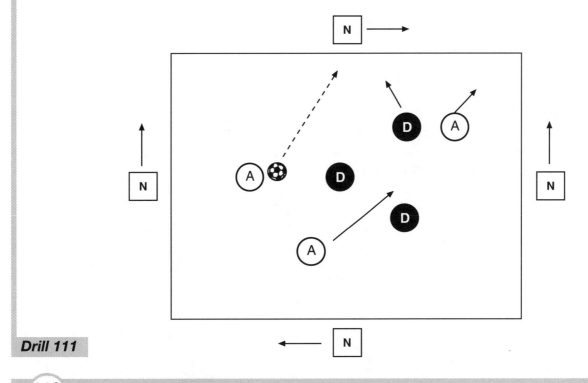

Drill 111

112 Pass to the End Zone

Purpose

To practice passing and receiving skills under game-simulated pressures of restricted space, limited time, and challenging opponents.

Organization

Outline a playing area of 30 by 50 yards. Designate two end zones 10 yards deep spanning the width of the field. Organize two teams of four players each; both teams station themselves in the central area of the field (between the end zones). Each team defends an end zone; there are no goals or goalkeepers. Award one team possession of the ball to begin.

Procedure

1. Begin with a kickoff from the center of the field.
2. Regular soccer rules apply except for the method of scoring.
3. Award one point for a pass successfully completed into the opponent's end zone.

continued

4. Defending players *may not* enter their end zone to intercept passes; however, they should take positions to block passing lanes and prevent the ball from entering their end zone.

5. Change of possession occurs when a defending player steals the ball, the ball goes out of play last touched by a member of the opposing team, and after a point is scored.

6. Play for 20 minutes.

7. The team scoring the most points wins.

Key Points

- Player must move off the ball to create passing options.
- Emphasize the importance of the first touch to create time and space when receiving the ball.
- Emphasize proper support movement.

Variations

- Designate smaller end zones for higher-level players (to increase scoring difficulty).
- Impose restrictions on players (for example, limit players to three or fewer touches to control and pass the ball).

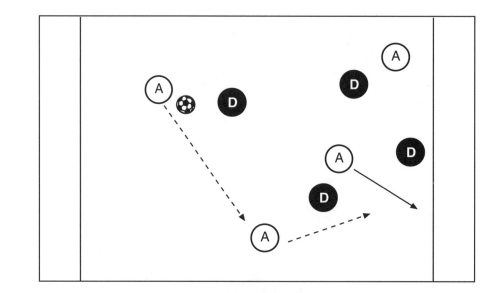

Drill 112

113 Pass and Receive to Score

Purpose

To practice passing and receiving skills under game-simulated pressures and to improve decision making.

Organization

Play within an area of approximately 40 yards square. Use markers to represent six small goals (3 yards wide) positioned randomly within the field area. Organize two equal teams of four to six players each. Use colored scrimmage vests to differentiate teams. Award one team possession of the ball to begin.

continued

Procedure

1. Teams can score in all six goals and must defend all six goals.
2. Players score by passing the ball through either side of a goal to a teammate positioned on the other side.
3. Goals may not be scored consecutively through the same goal.
4. Change of possession occurs when the defending team steals the ball or when the ball is kicked out of bounds last touched by the attacking team.
5. Play for 20 minutes; regular soccer rules are in effect other than the method of scoring and waiving of the offside rule.

Key Points

- Players should read and react to defensive pressure and attack the goals least defended.
- Players must take proper support positions to create scoring (passing) options for the player with the ball.

Variations

- Require one-on-one marking to reduce the available time and space.
- Increase the goal size for beginning players; decrease the size for advanced players.
- Impose restrictions on players (for example, limit number of touches permitted to control and pass the ball).

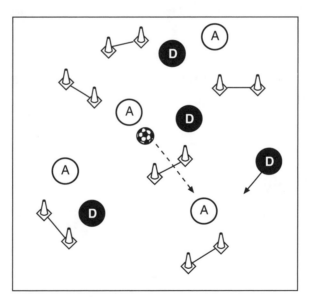

Drill 113

114 No Contact Passing and Receiving Game

Purpose

To improve group passing combinations.

Organization

Play on a 50-by-60-yard field. Position a small goal (4 yards wide) at each corner of the field. Divide players into two equal teams of six to eight players each. Use colored vests

continued

to differentiate teams. Do not use goalkeepers. Award one team possession of the ball to begin.

Procedure

1. Begin with a kickoff from the center of the field.
2. Regular soccer rules apply except for the following restrictions:
   - Players are limited to three or fewer touches to control, pass, and shoot the ball.
   - Defending players gain possession of the ball by intercepting opponent's passes or when the ball is played out of bounds last touched by an opponent.
   - Tackling the ball from an opponent is prohibited.
3. Each team defends the two goals positioned on its end line and attacks the two goals positioned on the opponent's end line.
4. Teams score by passing the ball through an opponent's goal.
5. Award one point for a goal scored or for eight consecutive passes without loss of possession.
6. Play for 25 minutes; the team scoring the most points wins.

Key Points

- Attacking players should position themselves to spread the defense.
- Encourage quick ball movement to change the point of attack and unbalance the defense.
- Emphasize passing and receiving efficiency. Skillful players will create more time and space for themselves and their teammates.

Variations

- Reduce area size to limit the time and space available to players.
- Adjust the number of touches permitted to pass and receive the ball.
- Adjust the method of scoring to accommodate the age and ability of players.

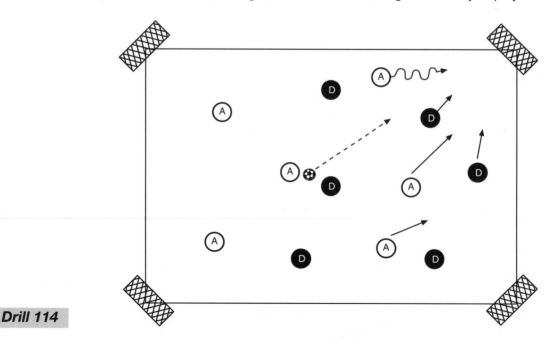

Drill 114

115 6 vs. 4 Possession Game

Purpose

To develop passing and receiving skills in a game-simulated situation.

Organization

Designate a team of six players team A and a team of four players team D. Use markers to outline a field area of 40 by 50 yards. Award team A possession of the ball to begin.

Procedure

1. Team A attempts to keep the ball from team D.
2. Team A players are restricted to three or fewer touches to receive and pass the ball.
3. Team D players, because they are outnumbered, have no touch restriction.
4. Award team A one point for eight or more consecutive passes.
5. Award team D one point each time one of its players steals the ball and dribbles out of the field area.
6. Team A players must prevent team D players from dribbling out of the area.
7. Play for 20 minutes.
8. The team scoring the most points wins.

Key Points

- The attacking team must use the entire width and length of the area to create open space and passing lanes.
- Team A players should adjust their positions to the movement of the ball and location of supporting teammates. The overall shape of the team is dynamic, ever changing.
- Encourage quick ball movement to draw opponents out of position.

Variation

Adjust the size of the area depending on the age and ability of players (reduce space for higher-level players; increase space for beginners).

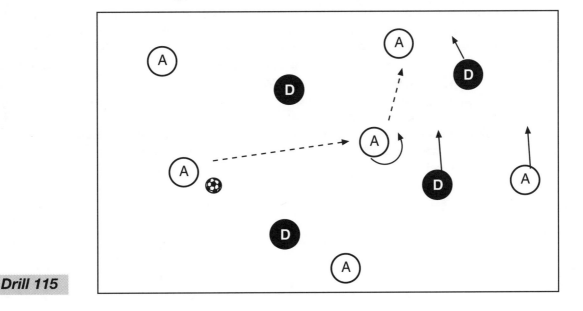

Drill 115

12
Dribbling Skills

Joe Luxbacher
University of Pittsburgh

Dribbling in soccer serves much the same function as dribbling in basketball—it enables players to advance (penetrate) with the ball while maintaining possession from opponents. Unlike other soccer skills, dribbling techniques may differ from one player to the next. Individuals can develop their own dribbling style and personality as long as they achieve the primary objective of beating opponents while maintaining possession of the ball. Dribbling skills are used to best advantage in the attacking third of the field nearest the opponent's goal. If an attacking player can successfully take on (dribble past) an opponent in that area, then he or she has created a scoring opportunity or at least a situation that can lead to a scoring opportunity. Players should limit dribbling in the middle and defending thirds of the field where loss of possession can result in a goal against.

Dribbling is sometimes considered an art rather than a skill because individuals can express themselves in different ways. Some players dribble with short, choppy steps, keeping the ball very close to their feet. Others prefer longer, smoother strides. Some rely solely on deceptive foot movements and body feints to unbalance opponents. Others employ quick bursts of speed and sudden changes of direction. What works for one player may not work for another.

Individual differences aside, players commonly use two general dribbling techniques in game situations. Players *dribble for close control*, keeping the ball close to their feet, in areas of restricted space where opponents are positioned to challenge for the ball. In contrast, players *dribble for speed* when advancing with the ball in open space, where straight-out speed takes priority over close control of the ball. Rather than keeping the ball close to the feet, the dribbler pushes the ball forward several steps, sprints to it, and then pushes it again.

116 Slalom Dribble

Purpose

To improve ability to change direction or speed while maintaining close control of the ball.

Organization

Divide players into teams of three. Position each team in single file facing a line of eight cones positioned one after the other three yards apart. Each team uses one ball.

Procedure

1. On command the first player in line dribbles at top speed through the slalom course, weaving in and out of the cones front to back to front.

2. On return to the starting line, he or she exchanges the ball with the second player in line, who in turn dribbles the slalom.

3. Continue until all players have dribbled the slalom course twice. The team completing the circuit in the shortest time wins the race.

4. Award 10 points to the first-place team, 8 points to the second-place team, and 6 points to the third-place team. Penalize teams 1 point for each cone bypassed or knocked over. Determine total points scored by subtracting the number of penalty points from the points awarded for the team's order of finish. Repeat the race several times. The first team to total 60 points wins.

Key Points

- Players should always maintain close control of the ball.
- Players should use various foot surfaces (inside, outside, instep) to contact the ball.
- Players should keep their heads up with vision on the field.

Variations

- Reduce the distance between cones.
- Increase the number of cones.
- Increase the number of repetitions.

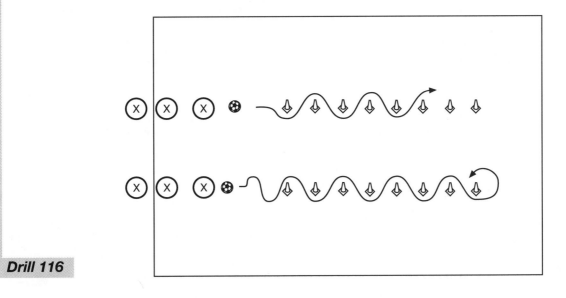

Drill 116

(117) Speed Dribble Race

Purpose

To improve dribbling speed and enhance aerobic capacity.

Organization

Play on one-half of a regulation field. All players, each with a ball, take positions an equal distance apart along the end line.

Procedure

1. On the command "go" each player dribbles at top speed to the halfway line, turns, and dribbles back to the end line.
2. The first player to cross the end line with control of his or her ball is the winner.
3. Run a minimum of 10 races with a short rest period after each race.
4. Award 10 points for first place, eight points for second place, and six points for third place.
5. The first player to total 100 points is the winner.

Key Points

- The dribbler should push the ball two or three yards ahead and sprint to it.
- Players should contact the ball with the outside surface of the instep.

Variations

- Increase or decrease the dribbling distance based on the age and ability level of the players.
- Add defenders, each one chasing a dribbler. The defender attempts to catch the dribbler and kick the ball away.

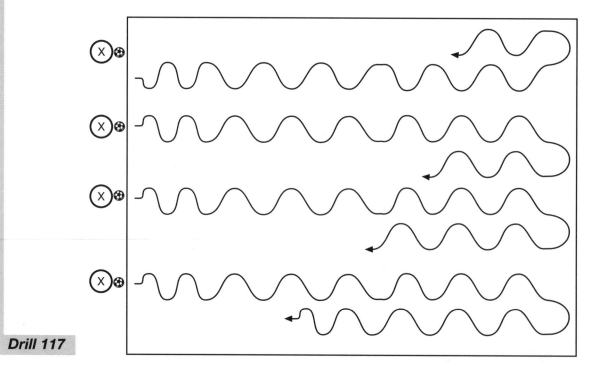

Drill 117

118 Shadow Drill

Purpose

To practice sudden changes of speed and direction, body feints, and close control of the ball when dribbling.

Organization

Outline a rectangular area of approximately 40 by 50 yards. Pair each player with a teammate. Each player uses a ball.

Procedure

1. Partners dribble randomly within the playing area, one leading while the other closely follows.
2. The trailing player attempts to mimic the dribbling movements of the leader.
3. Partners change positions every 60 seconds.
4. Play for 10 minutes.

Key Points

- The leader should use sudden changes of speed and direction coupled with deceptive dribbling maneuvers.
- Emphasize fluid, controlled movement with the ball.
- Partners should keep their heads up with vision on the field.

Variations

- Form groups of three or four players.
- One player dribbles, and the other follows without a ball. The trailing player tries to kick the ball away from the dribbler.

Drill 118

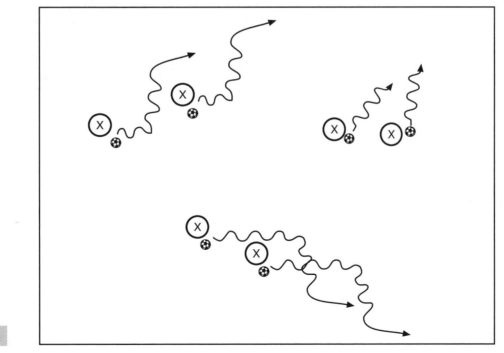

(119) **Change of Direction Drill**

Purpose

To incorporate sudden changes of speed and direction into dribbling style.

Organization

Position two cones approximately 10 yards apart on an end line or touch line of the field. Partners take positions on opposite sides of the line between the cones. One player has the ball.

Procedure

1. The player with the ball (attacker) attempts to dribble laterally to either cone before his or her partner (defender) can take a position there.
2. Players may not cross the line that separates them.
3. Award the dribbler one point each time he or she beats the defender to a cone.
4. Play continuously for 60 seconds (one round).
5. Players switch roles each round and repeat.
6. Play six rounds; the player who scores the most points is the winner.

Key Points

- Emphasize sudden changes of speed and direction to unbalance the defender.
- Players should use body feints coupled with deceptive foot movements.
- Encourage players to control the ball with various foot surfaces (inside, outside, sole).
- Players should maintain balance and body control by using a low center of gravity.

Variations

- Increase distance between cones.
- Position two cones at each end of the line to form small goals. The attacker scores one point by dribbling through either small goal before the defender can take a position there.

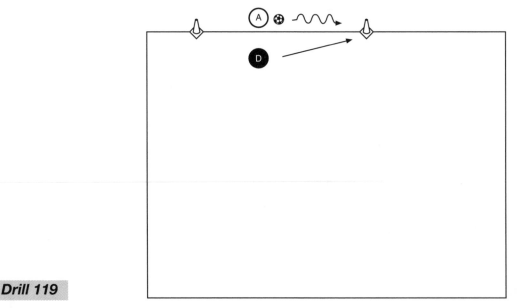

Drill 119

120 All vs. All

Purpose

To maintain possession of the ball from challenging opponents.

Organization

Outline an area of 30 yards square. All players, each with a ball, take positions within the area.

Procedure

1. All players dribble randomly within the field area while avoiding contact with other dribblers.
2. On a signal from the coach the game becomes all vs. all.
3. Each player protects his or her ball while attempting to kick other players' balls out of the area.
4. Slide tackles are prohibited.
5. A player whose ball is kicked out of the area is eliminated from the competition.
6. Eliminated players leave the area and practice juggling their balls until the game is over.
7. The game ends when only one dribbler remains in possession of a ball.

Key Points

- Players should combine dribbling and shielding skills to possess the ball.
- Emphasize sudden changes of speed and direction.
- Dribblers should keep their heads up with vision on the field.

Variations

- Decrease area size for experienced players; increase area size for beginners.
- Designate two players as defenders who take positions outside the area to begin. On the coach's command defenders enter the area and attempt to kick dribblers' balls out of the area. The defender who kicks the most balls out of the area is the winner. Repeat the game with two different defenders.

Drill 120

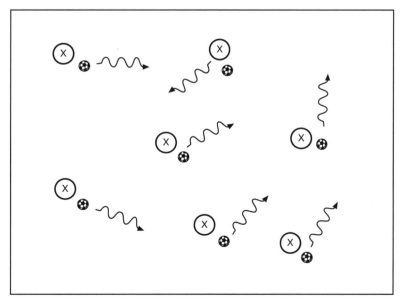

121   1 vs. 1 to Central Goal

Purpose

To improve ability to beat a defender in a one-on-one situation and to improve fitness.

Organization

Pair players for the competition. Outline a 20-yard-square playing area. Position two flags or cones in the center of the area to represent a small goal. Award one player possession of the ball.

Procedure

1. Partners compete 1 vs. 1 within the area.
2. Players score by dribbling through either side of the central goal.
3. Change of possession occurs when the defending player steals the ball or when it travels out of bounds last touched by the attacking player.
4. Players change roles immediately with each loss of possession.
5. Slide tackles are prohibited.
6. Play continuously for 90 seconds, rest, and repeat.

Key Points

- Emphasize change of speed when accelerating past the defender.
- Attacker should protect (shield) the ball when attempting to turn on the defender.
- Encourage immediate transition from attack to defense and vice versa on change of possession.

Variations

- Increase goal size for beginning players.
- Decrease duration of the game to 30 seconds for young players.
- Award points for passing through the goal as well as for dribbling through the goal.

Drill 121

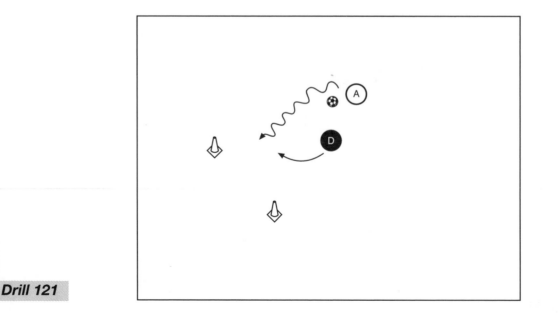

122 Take on Defender to End Line

Purpose

To improve ability to take on and beat a defender.

Organization

Pair each player with a partner. Outline a 20-by-30-yard playing area for each pair. Position two cones 4 yards apart to represent a goal at the midpoint of each end line. Each player defends a goal and can score in the opponent's goal. Award one player the ball to begin.

Procedure

1. Players take positions in their respective goals.
2. The player with the ball serves a lofted pass to his or her partner (attacker) and immediately moves forward from the goal to play as a defender.
3. The attacker attempts to dribble past the defender and through the goal.
4. Award one point for a goal scored.
5. Players return to their respective goals after each attempt and then repeat the drill.
6. Partners alternate playing as defender and attacker.
7. The first player to score 10 points wins the contest.

Key Points

- Players should use deceptive body feints to unbalance the defender.
- The attacker should dribble at the defender at top speed.
- The dribbler should take the most direct route to the goal.

Variations

- Reduce size of the playing area for younger players.
- Increase goal width to provide the dribbler a wider corridor in which to beat the defender.

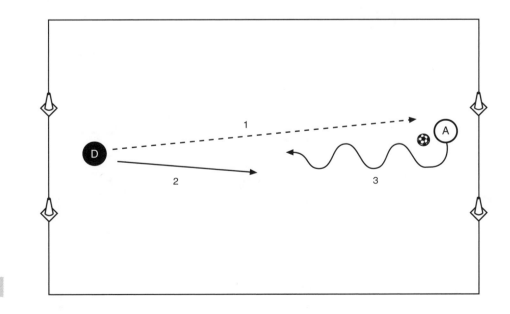

Drill 122

123 Four-Zone Game

Purpose

To improve ability to take on and beat a defender.

Organization

Four players participate. Use markers to divide a 10-by-40-yard field area into four consecutive 10-by-10-yard zones. One player (attacker) sets up in zone 1 with the ball; the remaining players each take a position in one of zones 2, 3, or 4.

Procedure

1. The player with the ball tries to dribble the length of the field while staying within the side boundaries.

2. Defenders, who are restricted to movement within their assigned zone, attempt to tackle the ball from the dribbler.

3. Once the attacker dribbles past the defender in a zone, he or she immediately advances to take on the defender in the next zone.

4. If a defender steals the ball, he or she immediately returns it to the attacker, who advances to take on the next defender.

5. After taking on the defender in zone 4, the attacker remains there to play as a defender in the next round.

6. Each of the original defenders moves forward one zone. The player who moves into zone 1 becomes the attacker for the next round.

7. Award one point for each defender beaten for a maximum of three points per round.

8. The player who scores the most points after 10 rounds wins the competition.

Key Points

- The dribbler should use deceptive body feints coupled with sudden changes of speed and direction to unbalance the defender.

- The dribbler should take on the defender at speed.

- The dribbler should maintain a low center of gravity and close control of the ball when dribbling.

Variations

- Decrease zone width to five yards.

- Increase the number of zones and defenders to six.

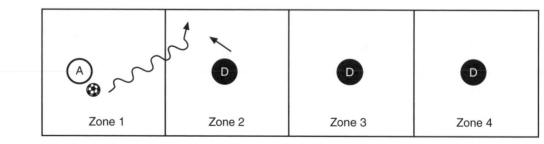

Drill 123

124 1 vs. 2 to Sideline

Purpose

To combine dribbling and shielding skills.

Organization

Use markers to outline a playing area of 20 yards square. Two players take positions within the area; one (attacker) has possession of the ball to begin, and the other defends. Station an additional player, a neutral defender, on each of the four sidelines. Neutral defenders attempt to prevent players from dribbling out of the area. Each neutral defender is free to move along the length of his or her sideline.

Procedure

1. Partners compete 1 vs. 1 within the field area.

2. The player with the ball scores one point by dribbling out of the area; his or her opponent prevents scores by stealing (tackling) the ball. Players immediately reverse roles upon change of possession.

3. Neutral defenders stationed along the sidelines assist in preventing attackers from dribbling out of the area. This creates a 1 vs. 2 advantage for the defense.

4. Play a series of two-minute games with one minute of active rest (for example, ball juggling) between games.

Key Points

- The dribbler should use sudden changes of speed or direction to unbalance the defender.

- The dribbler should keep his or her head up when dribbling.

Variations

- Position two neutral defenders along each sideline.

- Adjust the size of the playing area to the age and ability of the players.

- Group players in threes—one attacker vs. two defenders within the field area.

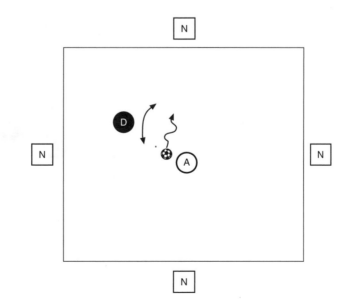

125 Four-Goal Game

Purpose

To develop dribbling and shielding skills in game-simulated conditions.

Organization

Use markers to outline a field area of 50 yards square. Position cones or flags to represent a goal 4 yards wide at the center of each sideline. Organize two teams of five players each. Award one team possession of the ball.

Procedure

1. Begin with a kickoff from the center of the area.
2. Each team must defend two goals and can score in the opponent's two goals.
3. Do not use goalkeepers.
4. Award a team one point for dribbling the ball through an opponent's goal.
5. Regular soccer rules apply except that the offside rule is waived.
6. Play for 25 minutes.

Key Points

- Dribblers should keep their heads up with vision on the field.
- The attacking team should unbalance the defending team by quickly changing the point of attack.

Variations

- Reduce the field size.
- Require strict one-on-one marking of all players.
- Add a neutral player who always plays with the defending team to give that team a numerical advantage.
- Position two additional goals within the playing area to provide dribblers with more scoring options.

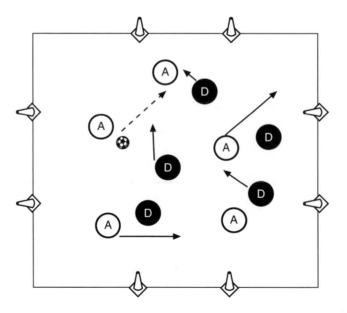

Drill 125

(126) Score by Dribbling Only

Purpose

To emphasize dribbling and shielding skills in an actual game situation.

Organization

Two teams of six play on a field area of approximately 40 by 60 yards. Teams score by dribbling the ball over the opponent's end line. The entire length of the end line is considered the goal. Use colored scrimmage vests to differentiate teams.

Procedure

1. Begin with a kickoff from the center of the field.
2. Regular soccer rules are in effect except for method of scoring.
3. Play for 20 minutes.
4. The team scoring the most points wins the game.

Key Points

- Players should always maintain balance and body control.
- Players should use sudden changes of speed or direction.
- Encourage players to take on opponents in the attacking third of the field.
- Players should not take on opponents in the defending third of the field.

Variations

- Decrease the width of the playing area to limit the available space.
- Add two neutral players who join the defending team.

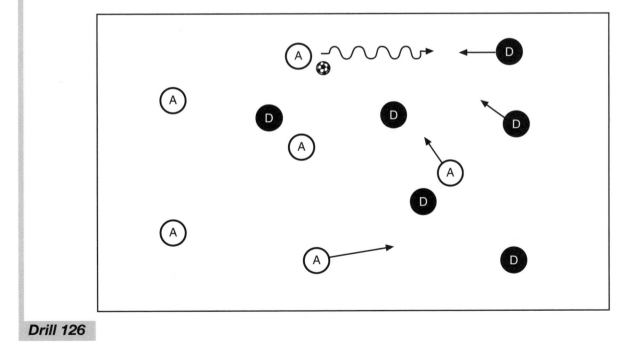

Drill 126

127 Dribbling Game (With Restrictions)

Purpose

To improve dribbling skills in a game-simulated situation with emphasis on dribbling in appropriate areas of the field.

Organization

Use markers to outline a 60-by-30-yard field with a regulation goal positioned on the center of each end line. Divide the field lengthwise into three equal-size (20-yard) zones. Form two teams of four field players and a goalkeeper. Award one team possession of the ball to begin.

Procedure

1. Begin with a kickoff from the center of the field.
2. Adopt the following zone restrictions:
   - Players may use only one- and two-touch passing in the zone nearest their goal (defending third).
   - In the middle third players may advance the ball by dribbling into open space but may not take on (dribble past) and beat opponents.
   - Dribbling is mandatory in the attacking third of the field. Players must beat an opponent on the dribble before passing or shooting on goal.
3. Violation of a zone restriction is penalized by loss of possession to opponents.
4. Teams score by kicking the ball past the opposing goalkeeper and into the goal.
5. Regular soccer rules apply.
6. Play for 25 minutes. The team scoring the most goals wins the game.

Key Points

- Limit dribbling in the defending third.
- Encourage dribbling in the attacking third.

Variations

- Reduce field size to restrict the space and time available to attacking players.
- Add a neutral player who plays with the defending team to give that team a numerical advantage.

Drill 127

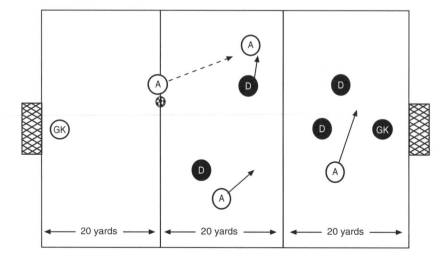

(128) 1 vs. 1 Marking Game

Purpose

To develop individual dribbling and shielding skills and emphasize tactical use of dribbling skills.

Organization

Form two teams of four players each. Use markers to outline a field area of 30 by 40 yards with a goal 4 yards wide positioned at the center of each end line. Do not use goalkeepers. Award one team possession of the ball to begin.

Procedure

1. Begin with a kickoff from the center of the field.
2. Each team defends a goal and can score by dribbling over the opponent's end line or shooting through the opponent's goal.
3. Require one-on-one marking of opponents.
4. Regular soccer rules are in effect.
5. Change of possession occurs when a defending player steals the ball, when the ball goes out of play, or when a goal is scored.
6. Play for 20 minutes; the team scoring the most goals wins the competition.

Key Points

- Emphasize tight marking.
- Attackers can penetrate the defense using the pass or dribble.
- Limit dribbling in the defending third of the field; encourage dribbling to beat the opponent in the attacking third of the field.

Variations

- Increase size of the playing area.
- Adjust goal size to accommodate the ability of players (reduce goal size for advanced players).
- Position two small goals on each end line to provide additional scoring options.

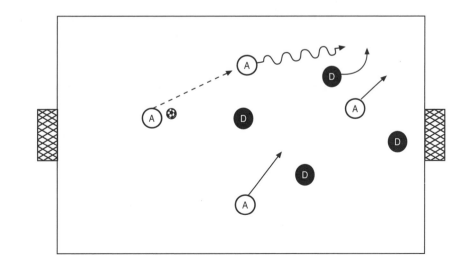

Drill 128

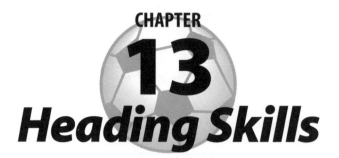

CHAPTER 13
Heading Skills

Joe Luxbacher
University of Pittsburgh

Soccer is the only sport where players literally use their heads to score goals, pass the ball to teammates, and clear the ball defensively. The heading drills provided here focus on finishing the attack. During a game scoring opportunities may come off crosses, corner kicks, free kicks, and long throw-ins. To capitalize on such opportunities, players must be able to head with both power and accuracy. The top strikers in the world are adept at scoring with their heads as well as their feet. A prime example is German international Oliver Bierhoff, who scored several spectacular goals with his head during the 1998 World Cup.

Players use two distinct heading techniques to score goals, depending on the situation. Attackers use the *jump header* to leap above an opponent who is challenging for the ball. The player should use a two-footed takeoff to jump up. He or she arches the upper trunk back from vertical and tucks chin to chest. The head is steady, and the eyes are open, focused on the ball. The upper body snaps forward, and the flat surface of the forehead meets the ball at the highest point of the jump. The ball is driven on a downward plane toward the goal line. The *dive header* is an acrobatic skill that players use to score off low, driven crosses. The player dives parallel to the ground with the head tilted back slightly. The flat surface of the forehead contacts the ball. The player extends the arms and hands downward to break the fall to the ground. The player should attempt to keep his or her mouth closed when heading the ball. An open mouth invites injury because an unexpected bump or push from an opponent may result in the player biting his or her tongue.

129 Rapid-Fire Heading

Purpose

To improve jump-header technique.

Organization

Arrange players in groups of three. Two servers, each with a ball, take positions 10 yards apart. The third player takes a position midway between the servers.

Procedure

1. The central player moves toward a server, who tosses a ball upward.
2. The player jumps up, heads the ball back to the server, turns, and immediately moves toward the opposite server, who tosses a ball upward.
3. The player jumps and heads the ball back to the server.
4. Continue the drill for a total of 50 headers.
5. Complete two rounds of heading for each player (100 repetitions each).

Key Points

Players should

- jump vertically using a two-footed takeoff,
- arch the upper body back from vertical,
- keep the neck firm and the chin tucked to the chest,
- snap the upper trunk forward at the waist,
- contact the ball on the center of the forehead,
- meet the ball at the highest point of the jump, and
- execute the drill at maximum speed without sacrificing correct heading technique.

Variations

- Beginners head from a standing position (without jumping).
- Increase distance between servers.
- Add a passive defender to challenge for the ball at 50 percent effort.

Drill 129

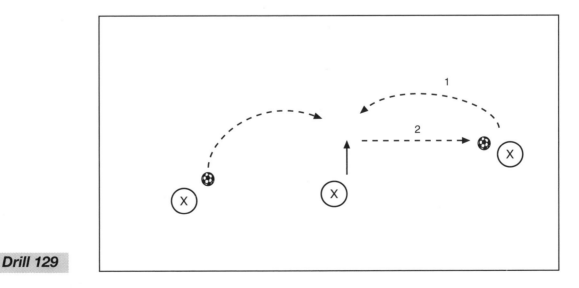

130 Throw-Head-Catch

Purpose

To improve jump-header technique.

Organization

Divide players into groups of three; number players 1, 2, and 3. Player 1 has the ball to begin.

Procedure

1. Players take positions 10 yards apart in a triangle.
2. Players jog throughout the field area while maintaining the 10-yard distance.
3. While jogging, player 1 tosses the ball upward. Player 2 jumps and heads the ball to player 3.
4. Player 3 catches the ball and tosses it to player 1.
5. Player 1 jumps and heads the ball to player 2.
6. Continue the throw-head-catch sequence until each player has headed 40 tosses.

Key Points

Players should

- use a two-footed takeoff to jump up,
- square their shoulders to the target, and
- contact the ball with the forehead, keeping eyes open and mouth closed.

Variations

- Increase distance between the players.
- Increase jogging speed.
- Add to the group a fourth player (defender) who challenges for the ball.

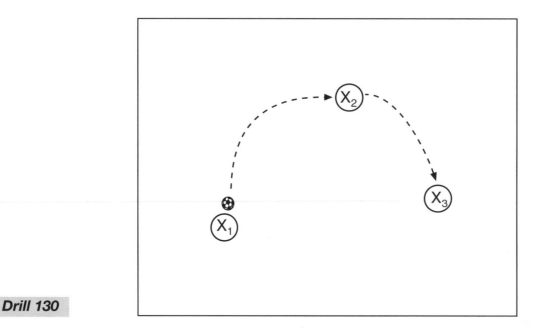

Drill 130

131 Dive Headers

Purpose

To develop dive-header technique.

Organization

Players pair with a partner and face one another at a distance of 10 yards. One player (server) has the ball to begin.

Procedure

1. The server tosses the ball parallel to the ground at approximately waist height toward his or her partner.
2. The partner dives parallel to the ground to head the ball back to the server.
3. Partners switch positions after 10 headers.
4. Perform two rounds of heading for each player.

Key Points

Players should

- dive parallel to the ground;
- tilt the head back, keep the neck stiff and eyes open, and contact the ball on the forehead;
- square their shoulders to the server when possible; and
- extend their arms and hands downward to cushion impact with the ground.

Variation

This drill is not appropriate for young children who lack adequate strength and confidence.

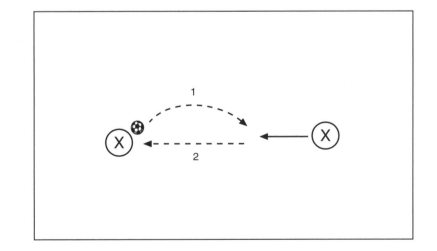

Drill 131

132 Heading to Score

Purpose

To develop ability to score goals from headers.

Organization

Divide players into groups of three. Use markers to outline an 8-by-12-yard area for each group. Position cones to represent a goal 4 yards wide on one end line. One player plays as a goalkeeper, one takes a position on a sideline of the grid as the server, and the third player sets up on the end line opposite the goalkeeper. One ball is required for each group.

Procedure

1. The server tosses the ball upward toward the center of the area.
2. The player on the end line moves forward to jump up and head the ball.
3. Award one point for a header on goal saved by the keeper and two points for a goal scored.
4. Players rotate positions after each header.
5. Continue the drill until each player has attempted 30 headers on goal.
6. The player scoring the most points wins the game.

Key Points

- Emphasize correct jump-header technique.
- Be sure that players head the ball on a downward plane toward the goal line when attempting to score.

Variation

Execute dive headers rather than jump headers.

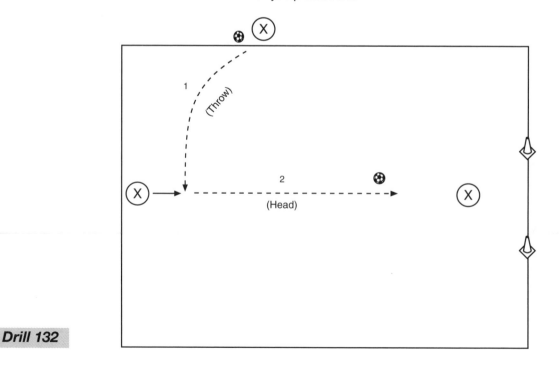

Drill 132

(133) Heading Goal to Goal

Purpose

To improve ability to score from headers.

Organization

Each player pairs with a partner. Use markers to outline a rectangular area of 10 by 15 yards for each pair. Position cones to represent a goal 6 yards wide at each end of the area. Partners set up in their respective goals; one has a ball to begin.

Procedure

1. A player tosses the ball upward toward the center of the area.
2. The partner moves forward and attempts to head the ball past the server through the goal.
3. The player may use a jump header or dive header depending on the trajectory of the ball.
4. Players return to their original positions after each header.
5. Repeat for 60 headers; partners alternate serving and heading.
6. Award one point for a ball headed on goal and two points for a goal scored.
7. The player totaling the most points after 60 repetitions (30 headers each) wins the competition.

Key Points

- Players should head the ball downward toward the goal line when attempting to score.
- Players should contact the ball at the highest point possible when executing a jump header.

Variation

Adjust goal size to accommodate age and ability of players.

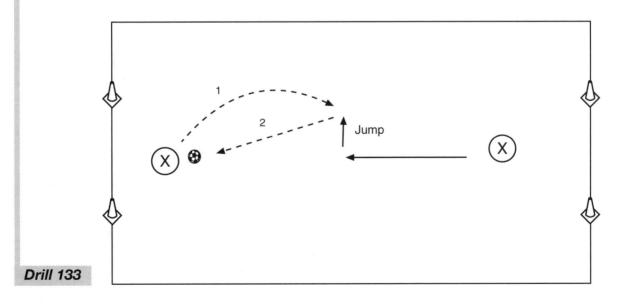

Drill 133

134 Score by Headers Only

Purpose

To improve ability to score off headers.

Organization

Use markers to outline a field area of 30 by 40 yards. Position cones or flags to represent a goal 6 yards wide at the center of each end line. Form two teams of four players each. Designate two additional players as neutrals who play with the team in possession of the ball.

Procedure

1. Each team defends a goal and can score in the opponent's goal.
2. Regular soccer rules are in effect except that the offside rule is waived and players pass and receive by throwing and catching, not kicking, the ball.
3. The coach begins play with a "jump ball" at center field.
4. The team gaining possession attacks; opponents defend.
5. Neutral players join the attacking team to create a 6 vs. 4 player advantage.
6. Players may take up to four steps with the ball before passing (tossing) to a teammate.
7. The defending team gains possession of the ball when
   - a defending player intercepts an opponent's pass,
   - an opponent drops the ball to the ground,
   - an opponent takes more than four steps when in possession of the ball,
   - an opponent plays the ball out of bounds, or
   - a goal is scored.

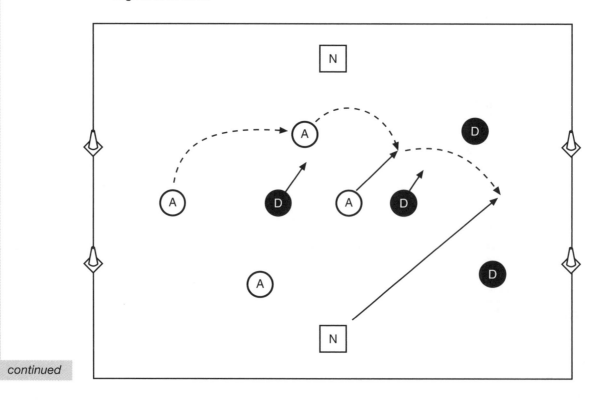

continued

8. Goals are scored by heading a tossed ball through the opponent's goal.

9. The drill includes no goalkeepers, but all players may intercept passes and block shots with their hands.

10. Defending players may not wrestle the ball from opponents.

11. Play for 20 minutes; the team scoring the most goals wins.

Key Points

- Players should head the ball on a downward plane toward the goal line.

- Players should use short, accurate passes (tosses) rather than long passes that have a higher risk of interception.

Variations

- Require scores by dive headers only.

- Use full-size goals with goalkeepers.

Drill 134

135 Scoring From Crosses

Purpose

To improve ability to score goals off crosses.

Organization

Play on one-half of a regulation field with a full-size goal positioned on the end line. Organize two equal teams of three or four players each. Team 1 (servers) sets up near one corner of the field with a supply of balls. Team 2 players set up on the opposite side of the goal area approximately 15 yards from the end line. A goalkeeper sets up in goal.

Procedure

1. Team 1 players alternate serving balls into the goal area.

2. Team 2 players attempt to score off crosses.

3. The goalkeeper attempts to save all shots.

4. Award one point for a header on goal saved by the goalkeeper, and award two points for a goal scored.

5. Teams exchange position after 50 crosses.

6. The team scoring the most points wins the round.

7. Play best of five rounds.

Key Point

Players can use a jump header or dive header depending on the trajectory of the cross.

Variation

Initiate crosses from both flanks and from various points outside the penalty area.

continued

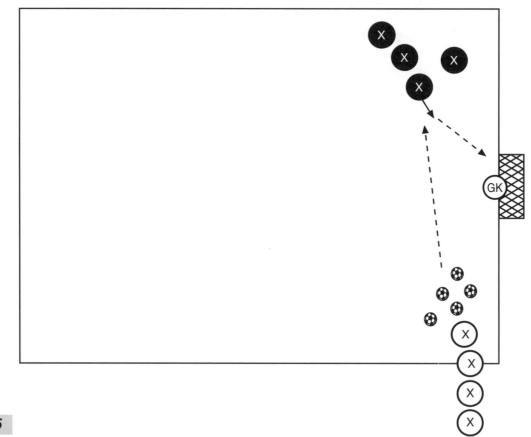

Drill 135

136 3 vs. 3 (+ 3) in Penalty Area

Purpose

To improve ability to score off headers.

Organization

Form three teams of three players each. Position two teams within the penalty area of a regulation field with a full-size goal positioned on the end line. Use cones or flags to designate three small goals (4 yards wide) positioned an equal distance apart on the outer edge of the penalty area. Designate one team as defenders and one team as attackers. Players from the third team function as servers. Position one server on each flank and the third server approximately 40 yards front and center of the goal. Each server has a supply of balls. A neutral goalkeeper sets up in goal.

Procedure

1. Servers alternate driving lofted balls into the goal area.

2. Attacking players attempt to head the ball past the goalkeeper.

3. Defending players try to outjump attackers and head the ball through one of the small goals on the edge of the penalty area.

4. Award the attacking team one point for a header on the large goal saved by the goalkeeper and two points for a goal scored with the head.

continued

5. Award the defending team one point for each ball headed through a small goal.

6. Teams switch roles after 20 serves (one round) and repeat the drill.

7. Continue until each team has completed two rounds as the attackers.

8. The team scoring the most points after two rounds wins the competition.

Key Points

- Emphasize proper timing of the jump.
- Players should head the ball downward to the goal line when attempting to score.

Variations

- Position two large goals on the end line.
- Do not use goalkeepers.

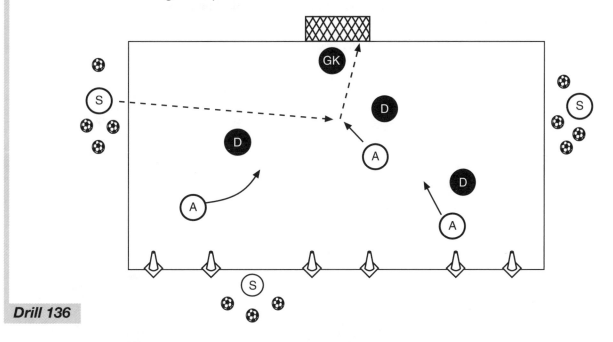

Drill 136

137 Game With Wingers

Purpose

To improve ability to score off crosses.

Organization

Use markers to outline a playing area of 60 by 45 yards. Position a regulation goal on each end line. Mark a zone 10 yards wide extending the length of the field on each flank. Organize two teams of four players each. Designate two additional players as neutral wingers who take positions in opposite flank zones. Position a goalkeeper in each goal. Award one team possession of the ball to begin.

Procedure

1. Begin with a kickoff from the center of the field.

2. Teams play 4 vs. 4 in the central field zone.

continued

3. The neutral wingers join the team with possession of the ball to create a 6 vs. 4 player advantage for the attacking team.

4. Wingers are restricted to movement within their zones.

5. Regular soccer rules are in effect except for the following restrictions:

   • All goals must be scored off crosses from wingers.

   • When a winger receives the ball from a central player or from the goalkeeper, he or she must dribble to the opponent's end line and cross the ball into the goal area.

6. Award one point for a ball headed on goal but saved by the keeper; award two points for a goal scored with the head.

7. Play for 25 minutes; the team scoring the most points wins.

Key Points

• Central players should delay their runs into the goal area until the ball is about to be served.

• This drill is also useful training for the goalkeeper in catching and controlling crosses.

Variations

• Allow goals to be scored from the general run of play as well as from crosses.

• Limit central players to three or fewer touches to receive and pass the ball.

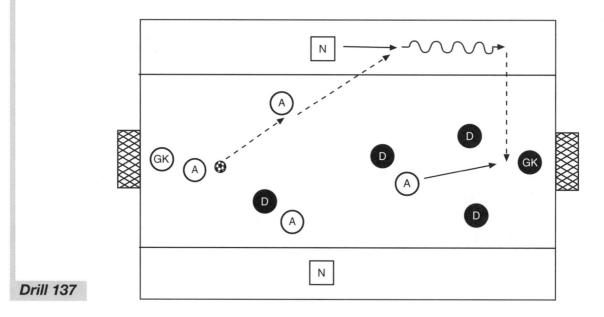

Drill 137

138 Multiple-Goal Header Drill

Purpose

To score from dive headers.

Organization

Form two teams of five players each. Play on one-half of a regulation field. Position cones or flags to represent six small goals four yards wide spaced randomly within the playing area. Do not use goalkeepers. Use colored vests to differentiate teams. Award one team the ball to begin.

Procedure

1. Passing and receiving among teammates is accomplished by throwing and catching, not kicking, the ball.
2. Teams can score in all six goals and must defend all six goals.
3. All goals must be scored from dive headers.
4. The ball may be headed through either side of a goal.
5. Defending players can prevent goals by intercepting passes or by blocking shots with their hands.
6. Attacking players are restricted to five or fewer steps when in possession of the ball.
7. Teams immediately switch from attack to defense upon change of possession.
8. Play for 20 minutes. The team scoring the most goals wins.

Key Points

- Emphasize correct dive-header technique. Players should dive forward with the body parallel to the ground and the head tilted back. Players should keep the head steady, contact the ball on the forehead, and cushion the fall to the ground with their arms and hands.
- Players should exercise caution to prevent midair collisions.

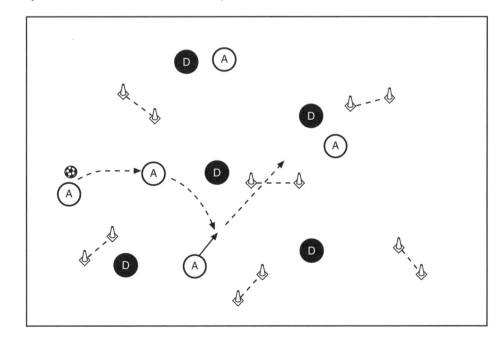

Drill 138

CHAPTER

14
Shooting Skills

Joe Luxbacher
University of Pittsburgh

Shooting skills are essential to finishing a successful attack. During the 1998 World Cup, players like Ronaldo of Brazil, Gabriel Batistuta ("Bati-gol") of Argentina, Dennis Bergkamp of the Netherlands, and Alessandro Del Piero of Italy garnered the most attention, and rightly so. These individuals and a handful of others possess the attributes—striking ability with either foot, composure under pressure, anticipation, determination, and supreme confidence—that enable them to succeed when most others fail. They are members of a select group of world-class goal scorers, the ultimate marksmen of international soccer.

Scoring goals is the single most difficult task in soccer. Success depends on several factors, one of which is the ability to shoot powerfully and accurately with either foot. Players use several shooting techniques, depending on whether the ball is rolling, bouncing, or dropping out of the air. The instep drive is generally used to strike a rolling or stationary ball. The full-volley, half-volley, and side-volley techniques are used to strike a bouncing ball or one that is dropping from above. The drills provided here expose players to the competitive pressures they will face in the game, pressures like restricted space, limited time, physical fatigue, and determined opponents. You can manipulate each drill to emphasize the shooting technique of choice or make the drill more or less difficult by adjusting variables in the training regimen. The more comfortable and confident your players become in executing shots, the more likely it is that they will demonstrate the physical and mental qualities required to take their goal-scoring abilities to the next level.

(139) Score Through the Central Goal

Purpose

To develop instep shooting technique.

Organization

Divide players into pairs. Position two flags 8 yards apart to represent a regulation-width goal for each pair. Partners take positions on opposite sides of the goal 50 yards apart. One player has the ball to begin.

Procedure

1. The player dribbles toward the goal, cuts right or left, and shoots from a distance of approximately 20 yards.
2. The partner retrieves the ball and attempts to score in similar manner from the opposite side of the goal.
3. Partners shoot back and forth through the central goal until each has taken 50 shots, 25 with each foot.
4. Award one point for a shot traveling through the goal below head height.
5. The player scoring the most points wins.

Key Points

- Emphasize correct shooting technique—kicking with the foot pointed down, foot firmly positioned, and the knee over the ball.
- Players should square their hips and shoulders to the goal as they strike the ball.

Variations

- Reduce goal width.
- A server plays the ball into the space in front of the shooter, who sprints forward and strikes the ball with his or her first touch.
- Add a chasing defender, who attempts to catch the shooter before he or she can shoot to score.
- Position a goalkeeper in the goal to prevent scores.

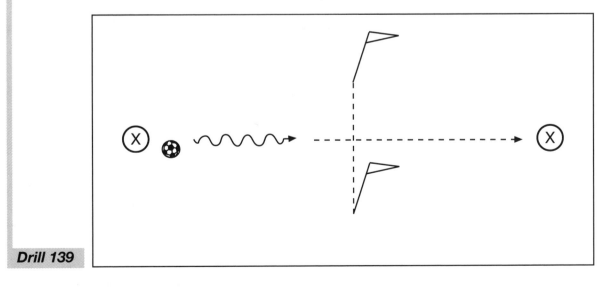

Drill 139

140 Pressure Shooting Drill

Purpose

To do repetitive shooting under pressure of player movement and physical fatigue.

Organization

Play on one end of a regulation field with a goal positioned on the end line. Three players participate—a goalkeeper, server, and shooter. The server sets up 30 yards front and center of the goal with a supply of balls. The shooter takes a position 25 yards from the goal facing the server (back to goal). The goalkeeper sets up in goal.

Procedure

1. The server tosses or kicks a ball toward the goal.
2. The shooter turns, sprints to the ball, and strikes it with one touch.
3. The shooter returns immediately to the starting position.
4. The server plays a second ball past the shooter, who turns immediately and sprints to the ball.
5. Shooting continues until players deplete the supply of balls.
6. The goalkeeper tries to save all shots.
7. Award one point for each shot on goal and two points for a goal scored.
8. Players rotate position after each round.
9. The player totaling the most points after five rounds wins the competition.

Key Points

- Players perform the drill at game speed.
- Emphasize correct shooting technique—shoulders and hips should be square to the goal.

Variations

- Vary the service by rolling balls, bouncing balls, and so forth.
- Alternate shooting between right and left feet.
- Add a defender to challenge the shooter.

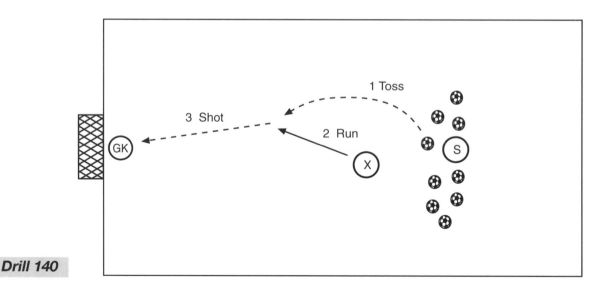

Drill 140

141 Toss and Volley to Goal

Purpose

To improve volley shooting technique.

Organization

Position a cone 25 yards front and center of a regulation goal. A player, the shooter, takes a position at the cone with a supply of balls. A goalkeeper sets up in goal.

Procedure

1. The shooter tosses a ball toward the goal, sprints forward, allows the ball to bounce once, and then volleys on goal.

2. The shooter returns immediately to the cone, picks up another ball, and repeats the drill.

3. The shooter continues until he or she depletes the supply of balls.

4. Award one point for each shot on goal and two points for a goal scored.

5. Repeat several rounds of shots with a short rest period between rounds.

Key Points

- Emphasize correct shooting technique—toe down, knee of kicking foot over the ball, head steady, and hips square to the goal.

- Execute the drill at game speed.

Variations

- Add a trailing defender to pressure the shooter.

- Require the shooter to shoot with both left and right feet.

- Have two additional players serve balls from various angles and locations.

- Have the shooter execute side-volley and half-volley shots.

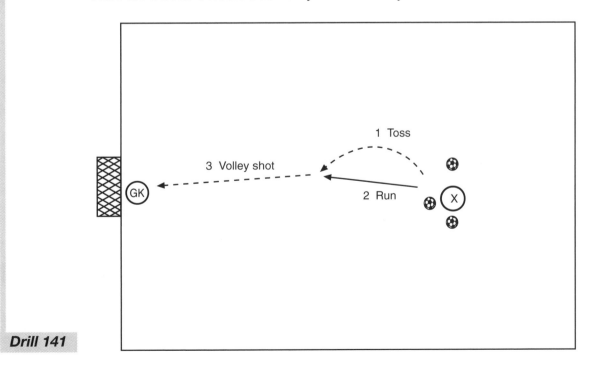

Drill 141

142   Goal-to-Goal Shooting Game

Purpose

To improve shooting accuracy and power.

Organization

Use markers to outline a 30-by-40-yard field. Center a regulation goal on each end line. Organize four groups (A, B, C, and D) of three players each; position one group next to each goalpost. A goalkeeper sets up in each goal.

Procedure

1. The first player in group A passes a ball diagonally to the first player in group B and sprints forward.
2. Player B receives and controls the ball, dribbles forward a few yards, and then lays the ball in the path of player A to shoot with one touch on goal.
3. Players A and B switch lines after the shot.
4. The first two players in groups C and D execute the drill from the opposite end line.
5. Continue until each player has taken 25 shots on goal.

Key Points

- Emphasize correct shooting technique—head steady, knee of kicking leg over the ball, kicking foot pointed down and firm, and ball contacted on full instep.
- Execute the drill at game speed.

Variations

- Impose a two-touch restriction on the shooter—the first touch to control the ball, the second touch to shoot.
- Have players serve lofted (bouncing) ball for the shooter to strike on goal.

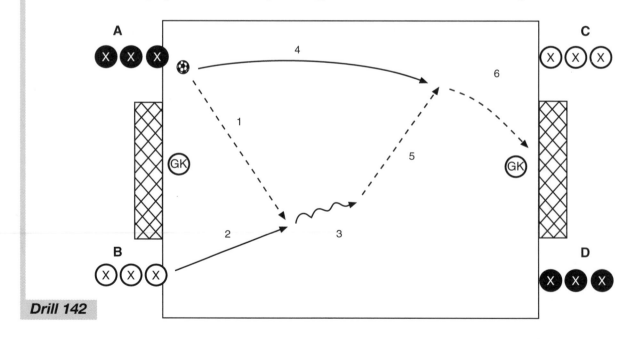

Drill 142

143   2 vs. 2 in the Penalty Area

Purpose

To improve shooting technique, fitness, and decision making in the attacking third of the field.

Organization

Play on one end of a regulation field with a full-size goal centered on the end line. Form teams of two. Two teams position themselves in the penalty area. A neutral goalkeeper sets up in goal and attempts to save all shots. A server sets up outside the penalty area with a supply of balls.

Procedure

1. The server kicks a ball into the penalty area.
2. Players vie for possession; the team gaining possession attempts to score, and opponents defend.
3. Teams switch roles immediately upon change of possession.
4. After a goal, a goalkeeper save, or a ball traveling out of bounds, the server kicks another ball into the area and play continues.
5. Continue the drill until the supply of balls is depleted.
6. Award one point for each goal scored.
7. The team scoring the most points wins.

Key Points

- Emphasize shooting accuracy over power.
- Encourage players to shoot at every opportunity.

Variations

- Add a neutral player who plays with the team in possession, creating a 3 vs. 2 advantage for the attack.
- Add a neutral player who plays with the defending team, creating a numbers-down (2 vs. 3) situation for the attack.

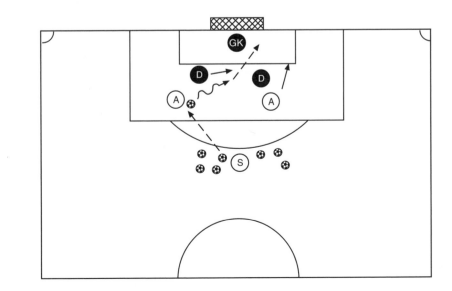

(144) Breakaway and Score

Purpose

To improve ability to score on a breakaway.

Organization

Play on one-half of a regulation field with a full-size goal centered on the end line. Mark a line parallel to the goal at a distance of approximately 35 yards. Pair players with a partner; each pair uses a ball. Do not use a goalkeeper.

Procedure

1. Partners (players 1 and 2) line up side by side on the 35-yard line.
2. Player 1 pushes the ball toward the goal and sprints to it.
3. Player 2 remains on the starting line until player 1 touches the ball a second time and then sprints forward to catch player 1 to prevent a score.
4. Player 1 must dribble into the penalty area before releasing a shot on goal.
5. Players rotate positions after each attempt.
6. Award the shooter one point for a goal scored.
7. The player with the most points after 20 repetitions wins the competition.

Key Points

- The player with the ball must dribble at top speed.
- The dribbler should follow the most direct route to the goal.

Variations

- Position a goalkeeper to save shots.
- Serve bouncing balls toward the goal and require volley shots.

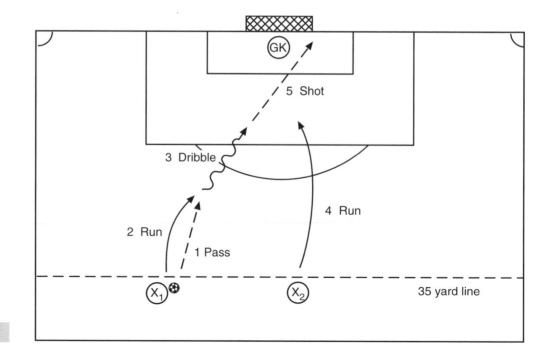

Drill 144

(145) Long-Distance Shooting Game

Purpose

To develop the ability to shoot with power and accuracy from outside the penalty area.

Organization

Use markers to outline a playing area of 45 by 60 yards. Position a regulation-size goal at the midpoint of each end line. Divide the field lengthwise into three 20-yard zones. Organize two teams of five players each; position a goalkeeper in each goal. Award one team the ball to begin.

Procedure

1. Begin with a kickoff from the center of the field.
2. Each team defends a goal and attempts to score in the opponent's goal.
3. Regular soccer rules apply except that all shots must be taken from the middle zone (20 yards or farther from the goal).
4. Award one point for a shot on goal saved by the goalkeeper; award two points for a goal scored.
5. Play for 25 minutes. The team scoring the most points wins.

Key Points

- Encourage long-distance shooting.
- Emphasize proper shooting technique—hips and shoulders square to the goal, complete follow through of the kicking leg.

Variations

- Adjust the shooting distance to the age and ability of players.
- Place restrictions on players, for example, three or fewer touches to receive, pass, and shoot the ball.

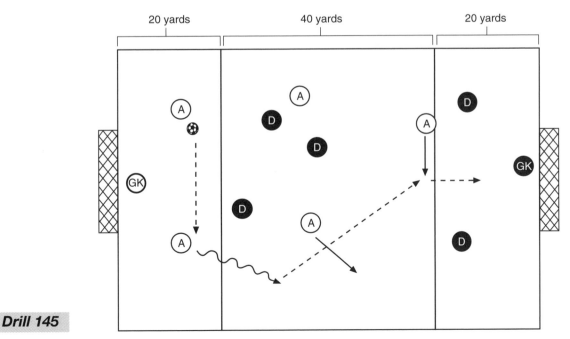

Drill 145

146 Score Off a Back Pass

Purpose

To develop instep shooting technique.

Organization

Play on one end of a regulation field with a full-size goal centered on the end line. Organize two teams of three players each plus one neutral player. Position a goalkeeper in the goal. Use colored vests to differentiate teams and the neutral player. Award one team the ball to begin.

Procedure

1. The neutral player joins the team in possession to create a 4 vs. 3 advantage for the attack.

2. Regular soccer rules apply except for method of scoring. Goals can be scored only from shots of a ball passed back out of the penalty area.

3. Award one point for a shot on goal saved by the goalkeeper; award two points for a goal scored.

4. After each goal or goalkeeper save, the keeper restarts play by throwing or kicking the ball to a corner of the playing field where teams vie for possession.

5. Play for 20 minutes; the team scoring the most goals wins the competition.

Key Points

- Players should position at wide angles of support.
- Emphasize power and accuracy of shots.

Variations

- Reduce size of the field area for younger players.
- Use two neutral players to create a greater advantage for the attacking team.

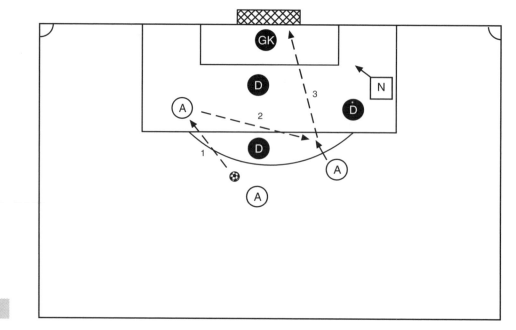

Drill 146

147 Two-Zone Shooting Game

Purpose

To improve shooting technique.

Organization

Play on a field area of 60 by 40 yards bisected by a midline. Designate two teams of five field players and a goalkeeper for each. Position a regulation goal on each end line. Designate three attackers and two defenders for each team. Attackers station themselves in the opponent's half of the field; defenders take positions in their half (nearest their goal). This setup creates a 3 vs. 2 situation in each zone. Station a goalkeeper in each goal. Use colored vests to differentiate teams. Award one team possession of the ball.

Procedure

1. Each team defends a goal and can score in the opponent's goal.
2. Attackers and defenders are restricted to their designated zones.
3. A defender who wins the ball initiates a counterattack by passing to a teammate (attacker) in the opponent's half of the field.
4. After each save the goalkeeper distributes the ball to one of the defenders in the defending zone.
5. The team scored against is awarded possession of the ball to restart play.
6. Play for 25 minutes; the team scoring the most goals wins.

Key Point

Encourage players to shoot at any opportunity.

Variations

- Add an extra attacker to each team to create a 4 vs. 2 situation in the attacking zones.
- Impose restrictions, for example, two-touch passing only, one-touch shooting.

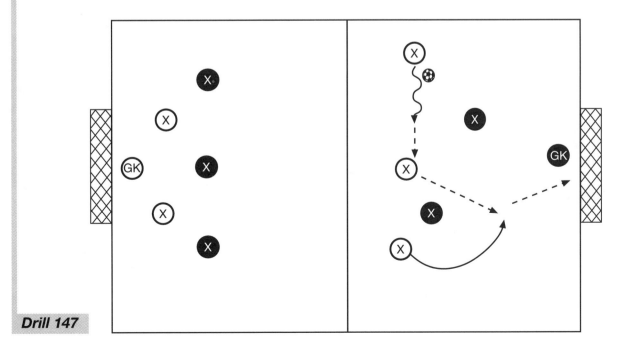

Drill 147

148 2 vs. 2 on Shortened Field With Full Goals

Purpose

To improve ability to shoot with power and accuracy.

Organization

Use markers to outline a 25-by-35-yard field with a full-size goal centered on each end line. Organize teams of two players each. Station a goalkeeper in each goal. Award one team possession of the ball. Position a server outside the area with a supply of balls.

Procedure

1. Each team of two players defends a goal and can score in the opponent's goal.
2. A server initiates play by kicking a ball into the field area.
3. The team gaining possession attacks; opponents defend.
4. After each shot on goal the server immediately kicks another ball into the field area.
5. Continue the drill until the supply of balls is exhausted.
6. Award one point for each shot on goal and two points for a goal scored.
7. The team scoring the most points wins the game.

Key Point

Encourage players to shoot at every opportunity.

Variation

Add a neutral player who joins the attacking team to create a 3 vs. 2 player advantage.

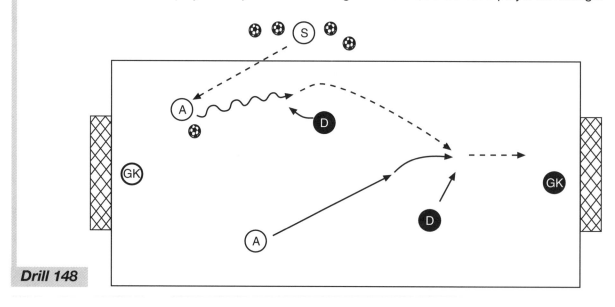

Drill 148

149 Volley Shooting Game

Purpose

To improve volley shooting technique under game-simulated conditions.

Organization

Designate two teams of four players each. Outline a field area of 35 by 45 yards. Center a regulation-size goal on each end line. Use colored scrimmage vests to differentiate teams. Do not use goalkeepers.

Procedure

1. Passing and receiving is accomplished by throwing and catching, not kicking, the ball.
2. Begin with a jump ball (similar to basketball) at the center of the field.
3. Each team defends a goal and scores in the opponent's goal.
4. Players can take a maximum of four steps with the ball before releasing it to a team-mate.
5. Change of possession occurs when a defending player intercepts a pass, the ball travels out of play, the ball is dropped to the ground, a player takes too many steps with the ball, or a goal is scored.
6. Players score by volleying a teammate's pass (toss) out of the air and into the opponent's goal.
7. Play for 25 minutes.
8. The team scoring the most goals wins.

Key Points

- Emphasize volley shooting technique—foot pointed down and firm, knee of the kicking leg over the ball, balance leg flexed, head steady.
- The ball should travel parallel to the ground, not diagonally upward.

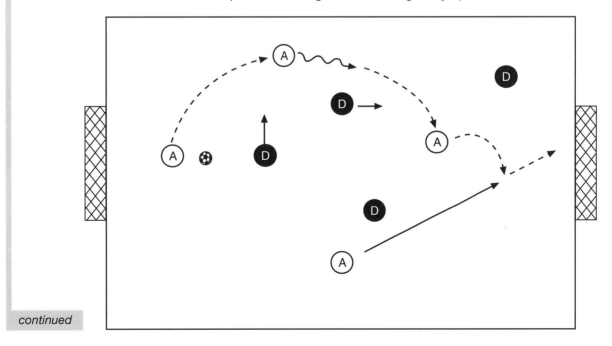

continued

Variations

- Add two neutral players who play on the team in possession to create a 6 vs. 4 advantage for the attack.
- Use goalkeepers with advanced players.

Drill 149

⑮⓪ 3 vs. 3 to Three Goals

Purpose

To do repetitive shooting under game conditions.

Organization

Play on a 30-by-40-yard field. Use cones or flags to represent three full-size goals on each end line. Position goals an equal distance apart. Organize four teams of three players each. Two teams compete at a time; players from the remaining teams play as goalkeepers, one in each of the six goals.

Procedure

1. Award one team possession of the ball.
2. Begin with a kickoff from the center spot.
3. Each team defends three goals and can score in the opponent's goals.
4. Play is continuous; teams reverse roles immediately upon change of possession.
5. Award one point for a shot on goal and two points for a goal scored.
6. Play five-minute games; the team scoring the most points wins the contest.

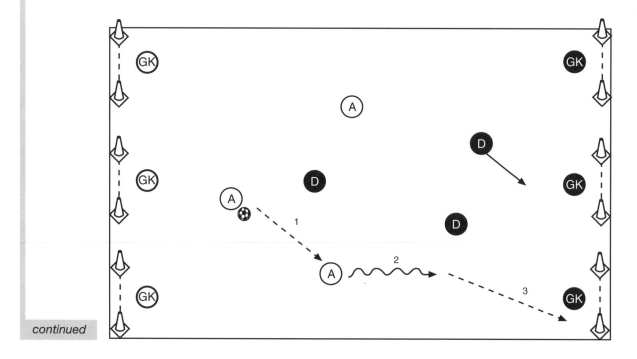

continued

7. Teams rotate positions after each game—goalkeepers take the field and field players become goalkeepers.

8. Play a series of five-minute games.

Key Point

Encourage players to shoot at every opportunity.

Variation

Add a neutral player who plays with the team in possession.

Drill 150

About the Contributors

Joe Luxbacher has more than 30 years of experience playing and coaching soccer at all levels. A former professional soccer player for the North American Soccer League, American Soccer League, and Major Indoor Soccer League, Luxbacher is head soccer coach at the University of Pittsburgh, a position he has held since 1984.

He was named Big East Athletic Conference Coach of the Year in 1992 and 1995, and he was selected for the Beading Soccer Club Hall of Fame in 1995. Luxbacher earned his PhD from the University of Pittsburgh in 1985 with specializations in physical education and management as well as administration of athletics. He lives in Pittsburgh, Pennsylvania.

John Astudillo has been coaching collegiate, national, and professional players for 18 years. His current reign as head coach of the men's soccer program at the University at Buffalo began in 1989. Since that time he has received five Coach of the Year awards and led his team to many postseason tournaments, including an Eastern Division championship in the Mid-Continent Conference in 1994. He also has coached the Empire States Games Western Scholastic team, winning two gold, four silver, and three bronze medals.

Dean Foti has been men's head soccer coach at his alma mater, Syracuse University, since 1991. He has served as the president of The Big East Conference Soccer Coaches' Association, has been a member of the NSCAA Regional Rating Committee (New York), and has served on the NCAA Regional Advisory Committee for the NCAA Division I Men's Soccer Championship. Before his coaching career, Foti was a starting player for the Orangemen for four years. During this time, his team was the inaugural Big East Tournament Champions in 1982, and he was named to the Big East Conference All-Tournament Team that same year.

Jay Hoffman holds the positions of assistant coach of the U.S. Women's National Team and Region I national coaching coordinator. He has helped lead the Women's National Team to three World Championship appearances and one CONCACAF Qualification appearance. He has been on the U.S. National Coaching Staff for over twenty years. Before his coaching began, Hoffman played on many teams, beginning with his college career in 1968 and ending with the MISL and NASL reserve teams in 1988.

Gene Klein is a United States Soccer Federation "A" licensed coach and currently serves as a United States Soccer Region I ODP staff member and assistant coach for the Pittsburgh Riverhounds. He also is coach of the Quaker Valley High School team and has helped them capture five Pennsylvania State titles. For his accomplishments, he was named NSCAA National Coach of the Year in 1996 and holds an Advanced National Diploma awarded by the National Soccer Coaches Association of America.

Samuel Koch has over 13 years of head coaching experience. He currently holds the position of men's head soccer coach at the University of Massachusetts. From 1991 to 1997, Koch has brought this team to a 79-45-13 record. He has been awarded two Atlantic 10 Coach of the Year awards, a New England Coach of the Year award, and a Pacific Soccer Conference Coach of the Year award. He holds a United Stated Soccer Federation "A" license and a National Soccer Association of America Advanced National Diploma. Before his coaching career, Koch was a four-year letter winner at Colby College.

John Kowalski spent ten years coaching the United States National Indoor Team before taking on his current position as head coach of the Pittsburgh Riverhounds. He coached the U.S. National Indoor Team to the bronze medal in 1989, the silver medal in 1992, at the FIFA World Championships, and the gold medal in CONCACAF in 1991. Coaching at Robert Morris College from 1989 to 1996, Kowalski helped lead this NCAA Division I team to four Northeast Conference championships. Prior to his coaching career, Kowalski was a player for many years, starting with four years at the University of New Haven and moving on to the New Britain Falcons, the Cincinnati Kids, and the Connecticut Yankees.

Stephen Locker, former head coach at Harvard University, led the Crimson to two NCAA Tournament appearances and two Ivy League titles. Locker has seen coaching success at Colgate University, Penn State, Otterbein College, and the University of Rochester. He holds a professional coaching license from the German Soccer Federation and played professionally for the German team, Hanover 96.

Dave Masur is currently the head coach of the men's soccer program at St. John's University. Since his arrival in 1991, he has guided the Red Storm to four regular season championships, five Big East Tournament Championships, and seven NCAA Tournament appearances. In addition to his shining coaching career, Masur was a very accomplished player. Highlights of his playing career include his induction into the Rutgers University Olympic Sports Hall of Fame; having his jersey retired in 1989 by Rutgers; and playing professionally with the Chicago Sting, the Toledo Pride, and the New Jersey Eagles.

Ronald Quinn has been head women's soccer coach at Xavier University since 1993. Quinn led his team to six straight winning seasons, including an Atlantic 10 Championship and a NCAA Tournament berth. In addition, he is a member of the United States Soccer Federation National Coaching Staff and a contributor to the development of the National Youth Coaching License and State Youth Modules.

David Sarachan has been assistant coach for DC United since 1997. Sarachan also has coached at Cornell University, leading the Big Red to two NCAA Tournament appearances. Prior to his coaching career, he played for the Big Red and also played two years at Monroe (NY) Community College, where he was a two-time All-American. He played professionally with the Rochester Lancers, Pittsburgh Spirit, Buffalo Stallions, Baltimore Blast, and Kansas City Comets.